CIVIC CENTER

PRAISE FOR *IMPACT*

"With *Impact*, Tim Irwin gives us deep thinking about a topic too often ignored—the guts to lead. We each have the ability, if we choose to take the leap."

—Seth Godin, author of *The Icarus Deception*

"Dr. Tim Irwin has another great story to tell in his new book, *Impact*. It is an excellent read that focuses us on the core values and foundational issues needed to sustain a leader in today's difficult business environment. *Impact* will cause you to think critically about who you are and what you're trying to accomplish."

—Michael L. Ducker, CEO and President, FedEx International

"Dr. Tim Irwin's new book, *Impact*, demonstrates how great leadership can make the difference between success and failure, and play an important role in improving the lives of others. Tim's analysis reinforces what I have discovered through experience: Purpose matters. People want to be part of something bigger than themselves. They want to make a difference in the world. Our job as leaders is to help people discover their Purpose, through self-awareness and self-examination find the Values that animate that Purpose, and from that understand one's Beliefs that drive Action. Tim's book is a wonderful 'how to' for any individual looking to take on this leadership task. In the end this journey is critical and urgent since it can improve our ability to make a positive difference in the life of another. What higher calling is there?"

—Robert A. McDonald, Chairman, President, and CEO (ret), The Procter & Gamble Company

"Tim Irwin underscores the ageless truth that sustained organizational excellence is as much, if not more, a function of the leader's character than of the leader's competencies. He provides thoughtful, practical, and meaningful ways for leaders to avoid the pitfalls of power and pride that too often bring down a leader. I recommend it to everyone, but especially to those leaders on the rise in their career."

—Dave Ridley, Senior Vice President, Southwest Airlines

"In *Impact*, author Tim Irwin digs deeply into the inner core of leaders to discover what enables them to succeed and why many derail. His revealing insights and constructive exercises provide you with many opportunities to overcome inner barriers and sustain your leadership. If you heed Tim's counsel, you will become a better leader."

—Bill George, Professor, Harvard Business School
and author of *True North*

"In my many years in the hospitality industry, I have worked with a number of very gifted leaders who had significant impact in their sphere of influence over a long period of time. While certainly they were highly competent, they had something else. Dr. Tim Irwin has written a powerful new book about that something else. He gives us the keys to having an impact and sustaining great leadership. I strongly urge you to read this book!"

—Horst Schulze, CEO and Chairman, Capella Hotel Group
(Formerly, Founding president and COO of Ritz-Carlton Hotels)

"Bravo! Tim Irwin's new book, *Impact*, hits on the key issue of our time: the crisis of leadership. Principled leadership from the 'core,' as Tim puts it, will be critical to putting our leaders and business ethics back on track. Tim has given us a great road map."

—Kevin Race, President and COO, Mortgage Banking,
J.P. Morgan Chase

"Finally, someone who knows and understands what leaders face every day gets to the core of it all in his new book, *Impact*. Dr. Tim Irwin challenges us to take a deep dive and understand what truly makes us tick as leaders. He follows this with practical suggestions that I for one implemented immediately, with visible results! This is all done with an entertaining and elegant penmanship that made me think I was paddle-boating down an easy river rather than reading what is truly a profound book. *Impact* is a must for anybody that wants to grow as a leader."

—Diana Derycz-Kessler, CEO, The Los Angeles Film School

"*Impact* should be required reading for anyone in leadership or aspiring to be. This book gets to the heart of what makes some leaders great and why others become catastrophic failures. I rarely find a book that I recommend to everyone I know—*Impact* is one of those."

—Wayne Huizenga, President, Huizenga Holdings

"Tim Irwin has written a very thoughtful and insightful book with great advice and counsel for every person leading or desiring the opportunity. I wish that it had been available to me early in my career as a leader. Sadly I had to learn some of his wisdom the hard way! What a great resource this is! A must read AND APPLY for every leader."

—David M. Ratcliffe, Chairman, President, and CEO of Southern
Company (ret)

"In his latest book on leadership, Tim vividly demonstrates why we want so much more from our leaders than simply running a successful team or organization. We want leaders to be 'profoundly trustworthy' and to inspire us to a higher sense of meaning and purpose in our work. If you aspire to be the kind of authentic, courageous, humble leader that people want to follow, you will find Tim's stories and insights to be most relevant."

> —**Bonnie P. Wurzbacher, SVP, Global Customer & Channel Leadership, The Coca-Cola Company (ret); Chief Resource Development Officer, World Vision, Int'l, London, UK**

"As CrossFit, P90X, or personal trainer-led work out regimens are for disciplined physical fitness enthusiasts, so *Impact* is for disciplined intellectual and emotional leadership enthusiasts. Through great insight, extensive application tools, and humor, Dr. Irwin helps the reader learn practical habits to strengthen and protect their core—their leadership core. If you are in leadership, or aspire to be, this is a must read!"

> —**Thomas K. Sittema, CEO, CNL Financial Group**

"Every leader is just one decision away from devastating failure. The only guardrail is the preparation leaders do ahead of time to know themselves, to set their principles, and to hold themselves accountable. Tim Irwin gives us a template for this soul journey. Use it well; get prepared; leave a legacy."

> —**Cheryl Bachelder, CEO, Popeyes Louisiana Kitchen**

"Dr. Tim Irwin has delivered a book that is practical, easy to read, and offers a high impact formula for great leadership. The world needs leaders who know what they believe and have the personal integrity and support systems in place to lead from their core. Irwin uses powerful illustrations and genuine solutions to identify, strengthen, and protect our core beliefs. Likewise, he uses real life examples of what can go wrong if we're not intentional in this important aspect of leadership. *Impact* is a must read for anyone serious about leadership."

> —**Brandon Barnholt, President and CEO, KeHE Distributors**

"I have witnessed both the positive and negative impacts that good and bad leaders can have on an organization. Unfortunately, the ramifications of bad leadership can be catastrophic. In this book, Dr. Irwin contrasts both good and bad leadership in a clear and practical way that provides a true roadmap for anyone interested in strengthening their managerial skills. Leaders in all areas of organizations will find Dr. Irwin's insights both foundational and relevant to navigating through today's career challenges."

> —**Walter Rakowich, CEO, Prologis (ret)**

"When you read Dr. Tim Irwin's latest book, *Impact: Great Leadership Changes Everything*, be ready to take notes and take action because meaningful self-revelations are on their way. I'd recommend leaders who want to make an impact read this one."

—Glenn A. Youngkin, CEO, The Carlyle Group

"Tim Irwin has a unique way of bringing out the best in leaders. He knows the key to having a lasting impact is how you treat people. Read *Impact* expecting to come away with new insights that will change how you approach leadership. This book is a must-read for every leader."

—Mac McQuiston, CEO, The CEO Forum

"Tim Irwin understands something we need to recognize every day: leadership is personal and comes from deep within our core. But how solid is that core when our potential impact as a leader is threatened? Read *Impact* and find out how to stay the course and protect your leadership legacy."

—Ken Blanchard, coauthor of *The One Minute Manager*® and *Leading at a Higher Level*

IMPACT

IMPACT

*Great Leadership
Changes Everything*

TIM IRWIN, Ph.D.

BenBella Books
Dallas, TX

New Yorker cartoons from www.cartoonbank.com on pages 25, 65, 152 used with permission, copyright © 2008 by David Sipress, 1992 by Lee Lorenz, and 2004 by Bruce Kaplan

BenBella Books, Inc.
10300 N. Central Expressway
Suite #530
Dallas, TX 75231
www.benbellabooks.com
Send feedback to feedback@benbellabooks.com

Printed in the United States of America
10 9 8 7 6 5 4 3 2 1

Library of Congress Cataloging-in-Publication Data
Irwin, Tim, 1949–
　　Impact : great leadership changes everything / Tim Irwin.
　　　pages cm
　　Includes bibliographical references and index.
　　ISBN 978-1-939529-04-6 (hardback) — ISBN 978-1-939529-05-3 (electronic)
1. Leadership.　I. Title.
　　HD57.7.I794 2014
　　658.4'092—dc23
　　　　2013034722

Editing by Debbie Harmsen
Copyediting by Eric Wechter
Proofreading by Chris Gage and James Fraleigh
Cover design by Brand Navigation
Illustrations by Matthew MacMillan
Text design and composition by Publishers' Design and Production Services, Inc.
Printed by Bang Printing

Distributed by Perseus Distribution
www.perseusdistribution.com

To place orders through Perseus Distribution:
Tel: (800) 343-4499
Fax: (800) 351-5073
E-mail: orderentry@perseusbooks.com

Significant discounts for bulk sales are available. Please contact Glenn Yeffeth at glenn@benbellabooks.com or (214) 750-3628.

To Anne,
a gifted leader

CONTENTS

FOREWORD

Once in a great while a book comes along that speaks directly and practically to the issues of the day. *Impact: Great Leadership Changes Everything* is one of those books.

The world is in desperate need of leadership. We need great leaders to find our way through the myriad of today's complex business and geopolitical challenges.

The problem is that many leaders are not having the impact they intend. They get in their own way and blunt the impact they could have. Often, it is not because they are not smart enough or knowledgeable enough of a particular issue. Instead they have drifted from the core principles that initially guided them as they moved through increasing levels of responsibility, authority, and power. They may have become arrogant or dismissive of the people doing the work of their organization and, at times, even their customers. They may sometimes exercise bad judgment about moral decisions. Inevitably, those leaders are marginalized to the point of irrelevance.

Dr. Tim Irwin's solution is simple but not easy. He offers practical tips to leaders to better understand and manage their internal decision-making process and judgments. This book is entertaining and profound at the same time. It is a fast read that calls out to be revisited and studied over and over again. One minute I was laughing out loud and the next I was reflecting deeply about my own life.

If it is your intention to exercise influence and make a difference with your life, then this book needs to move to the top of the reading stack on your bedside table. Irwin's principles provide a firm foundation for the weight of responsibility all leaders will bear, including future leaders. May it help you make the difference you intend.

Sincerely,
Mark W. Albers
Senior Vice President
Exxon Mobil Corporation

PREFACE

Leaders in all arenas—the corporate world, the military, government and politics, nonprofit organizations, and sports teams play a determinative role in whether human endeavors prosper, fail, or flounder. When an organization soars to greatness, we credit the leader. When it goes down, we usually blame the leader. We want our leaders to succeed. We need them to succeed. When they do, we trust them and follow them willingly. They inspire us to go the extra mile—to take our performance far beyond what we dreamed possible.

Most leaders want to make an enduring impact—a lasting and positive influence on the organization they lead and the lives affected by their decisions. Great leaders want to stay the course—to finish the race. Senior leaders have told me often that legacy is a far more powerful motivator than money.

Too often leaders fail to achieve a great legacy, and all are vulnerable to cataclysmic failures of leadership. Hardly a week goes by without some major leader going down and being vilified in the press. This does not even acknowledge the countless others who fail outside the media spotlight.

Why do some leaders make an impact, while others falter after initial success? Why do some endure all the perils and pitfalls leaders inevitably face, while others succumb to the seduction of power? Oddly, leadership failures rarely reflect a problem with the leader's competence. Most often the fall occurs because of a breach of something *inside the leader.*

My Commitment to You

In this book, we are going to look deeply at how what is inside a leader makes all the difference. We will learn how to strengthen what is inside in numerous positive ways. We might also view the time spent reading this book and applying its principles as a premium paid on our leadership insurance policies, so that we, too, do not go down that path of terrible destruction that so many have taken.

Impact is about the most important and serious dimensions of leadership, but this is not a somber book. I want us to take the principles seriously without taking ourselves too seriously. I provide many illustrations and tell a number of personal stories that I hope will not only be helpful, but also will make you laugh. Chapters are focused and relatively short. Most end with a "Go Deeper" section to give you a chance to slow down, reflect, and personally apply vital truths that have been discussed.

Impact reveals what it takes to be a strong, enduring leader and how we can protect ourselves from the foibles that bring so many promising leaders down. My commitment to you is that in the chapters ahead, this book will give you the keys to unlock the doors that lead to what so many of us want—to finish strong and to make an impact with our lives.

PROLOGUE

"Mr. Dennison, the board asked if you would please rejoin the meeting," Joan whispered to Doug across his massive desk.

"Hey, Matt, can you hold on for five seconds?" Doug Dennison put his hand over the mouthpiece and said, "Thank you, Joan, let me get off the phone with the analyst from IBD, and I'll be right over."

He continued his conversation: "Yes, Matt, as I mentioned on the earnings call two days ago, it looks like we will beat analysts' projections for revenue and earnings for the fourth quarter. I know in June we estimated mid-fifties per share, but it's likely going to come in around the low sixties. We had a couple of very good deals over the last sixty days with great margins. We'll say more about next year's outlook on the call in a few weeks. I'll try to give everyone some guidance then. Preliminarily, the outlook is good. Got to run back to the board meeting. Bye."

Doug walked down the mahogany wainscoted hallway, glancing at the stern portraits of Charigan Holdings' previous CEOs, who seemed like an empanelled jury of his peers. Why did his predecessors all seem so stoic? We've had a great year, and next year looks better, he thought. Leaving the boardroom during executive sessions of the quarterly board meetings always made Doug nervous, and some of the questions during the full session conveyed concerns on the part of some board members. At the beginning of the meeting three hours ago there were muted greetings, not the usual joking about one another's golf scores. But they had had a killer year on revenues and profits.

Then Doug pushed open one of the massive French doors of the boardroom. Several board members looked up, while others peered over their *gold-rimmed reading glasses at spreadsheets. Charigan's Board Chairman, Hal Barchans, greeted Doug and motioned him to the seat on his right.*

"Doug, during executive session, the board reached consensus that we need to make a change. We appreciate the financial results achieved this fiscal year, but the strategy to centralize all functions in New York is simply not working. There is an air of rebellion everywhere in the company. While the idea had great merit in theory and helped the bottom line this year, you did not win over the people most affected by the restructuring. You needed to get people with you on these decisions, and it just didn't happen. Many of our people know that senior management did not really support you on moving forward with implementation. You could have shown courage to reverse course when it was obvious you didn't have people with you, but you didn't. I think people's respect for you would have grown because it would have shown that you were listening. A lot of our best people are thinking about jumping ship.

"Your public hanging of Carl for opposing you on the changes created tremendous resentment in the field. Firing him was not the right answer. It seemed arrogant, petty, and mean-spirited to many, like you only wanted yes-men around you. When you were chosen to be the new CEO, the board had considered Carl and knew he could not do your job; however, the sales force loved him, and he got great results. There was an important role for him in our organization if you could have just worked out your differences. We think you should have figured out a way to win him over to your team.

"When we made you CEO, we talked about the values of Charigan. We affirmed how critical it was to live out the values so ingrained in our culture. We particularly stressed integrity in all our dealings and respect in how we treat our people. You enthusiastically endorsed them and promised to model them and to lead the company to follow them. While our values only identify the plumb line to which we all aspire, Charigan's corporate values were not exemplified in your behavior. Even though you achieved some impressive financial results for the company, we feel our great culture took a big step back since you took the helm. The board could not endorse your continuing as CEO.

"We're asking for your resignation, effective immediately. Joe Evans, our vice chair, will run things in the interim while we work out a succession strategy. You'll, of course, need a few days to get everything in order, and we want you to meet with a couple of us on Monday to work out the details of your departure. An announcement will go out this afternoon," Hal said with finality.

Doug looked around the room for a sign that someone might throw him a lifeline. "It sounds like there's no room to try to work this out," he said, absent his usual bravado.

Hal shot back, "Doug, this is a made decision. We appreciate your service to Charigan and wish you well going forward. The meeting is adjourned."

AN ALL TOO FAMILIAR TALE

Although this story is fictional, its narrative regrettably gets played out far too often in many organizations. When Doug assumed leadership two years before, he hoped he would make an impact. He really wanted to guide the company to new levels of prosperity and significance. Everyone from the chairman of the board to the guy in the mailroom had high hopes for Doug. The company needed a strong person at the helm who would lead Charigan into the future while preserving its rich seventy-five-year-old culture of taking great care of its people.

His departure will be noted in a short news item on *Fox Business* and in an article on page ten of the *Wall Street Journal*—nothing earth-shattering. After a year or two, Doug will likely land somewhere else as CEO. Charigan will survive the years of lost productivity and erosion of morale. What is hard to measure, however, is the impact to the collective psyche of the people of Charigan. The people who made Charigan a perennial member of American's Favorite Places to Work list just became cynical. They lost some of that edge of confidence that fueled competitive advantage in so many head-to-head battles with their marketplace rivals.

Charigan forfeited some of the great people like Carl who led with joy and infectious exuberance. Some who did not leave physically checked out emotionally.

Doug achieved some short-term financial results, but he damaged the organization that made it all work. His arrogance and abuse of power undermined his credibility and effectiveness as the leader. Could this have been prevented? Could there have been a different outcome? How great it would be to for this to be a redemptive story. Let's hold that thought. . . .

CHAPTER 1

MAKE AN IMPACT

"Guard your heart above all else,
for it determines the course of your life."[1]

—ANCIENT PROVERB

The outcome hung in desperate uncertainty. Whichever side won this battle would certainly win the war, and an obscure colonel unknowingly held the key to the now-famous battle.

Several weeks earlier, 120 members of the Second Maine Infantry Regiment laid down their arms in protest when a small group of their fellow soldiers were discharged from active service. Because of bureaucratic bungling some soldiers were mistakenly enrolled for a two-year enlistment and others for three. The three-year enlistees wanted the same treatment as their fellow soldiers, but the government would not permit them to be discharged from the army and return home. Filled with indignation, the men refused to fight. One officer declared them mutineers and wanted them shot. What their exact punishment would be remained in question, but for now they were detained as prisoners. The men from the Second Maine marched under guard to the camp of the Twentieth Maine regiment.

The conditions in the camp can only be described as dismal. The Twentieth, which originally formed with 1,621 soldiers, had suffered massive casualties and now fielded only 266 men. These remaining men were fatigued and sick, and some were wounded. The regiment remained critically short-staffed—the last thing they needed was to devote precious troops to guarding members of their own army. In fact, they urgently needed these 120 battle-hardened veterans to strengthen their depleted ranks and join them as comrades instead of prisoners.[2]

The colonel leading the Twentieth Maine regiment assumed charge of the prisoners and sought to rekindle their commitment to the North's cause. In a quiet, yet heartfelt and deeply personal speech, portrayed in the film *Gettysburg*, Colonel Chamberlain reminded the men why the Union army was fighting: not for money or land or personal advancement, but rather for the noble cause of setting other men free. The mutineers intently studied the face of the colonel and listened to his message. Slowly, all but four soldiers stood to convey their willingness to follow this man and to join in the fight.[3]

And so it was on July 1, 1863, that these two Maine regiments of Union soldiers set out together toward Gettysburg to risk their lives for a greater cause. The men's resolve and strength would be tested to the limit on day two of the battle in south-central Pennsylvania in a clamor to hold the vulnerable left flank. The Fifteenth Alabama Infantry Regiment, fully aware of the strategic importance of breaching the left flank of the Union line, bravely assaulted the hill again and again only to be thrown back.

The Union cannons and muskets fired down on the Fifteenth Alabama from behind large granite boulders that created a natural stronghold called Little Round Top. Acrid smoke from exploding black powder hung thick in the air. Savage screams from men killing one another at close range seemed darkly incongruent with the beauty of the rolling hills. The Twentieth Maine soldiers felt unspeakable dread, but they knew that if the Union's left flank collapsed, the North's line would certainly fail, and the battle would be catastrophically lost.

Colonel Chamberlain's troops, exhausted from holding off the repeated attacks on Little Round Top, ran out of ammunition. Chamberlain instinctively knew that they could not withstand another assault on their position. He was certain they must do something different, and he quickly revealed to his officers a new plan. They were to go on the offense, affix bayonets to their rifles, and move down the hill. The far left flank, which had almost doubled back on itself from the repeated attacks, would then swing around like a barn door. They needed to drive the Confederate forces back down the slopes of Little Round Top. The junior officers, clearly uncertain about this untested battle tactic, nonetheless trusted their leader. Sword drawn, the colonel led the assault down the hill.

Chamberlain and his forces drove the Confederates back, and the infamous Pickett's Charge near the center of the North's line became the focus of the battle. Union soldiers on a high ridge routed the Confederate troops as they attempted to cross a huge open field. The North won the Battle of Gettysburg, and it proved to be a crucial domino in the final campaign to end the war. Historians generally agree that if the South had prevailed in this battle, the nation would be strikingly different today.

The Power of Purpose

Lacking the background you would expect in a military commander, Colonel Joshua Lawrence Chamberlain was a sedentary thirty-four-year-old former college professor of modern languages from a family of strict moral values. Yet this inspirational, unflinching, quick-thinking leader changed the world forever. Recipient of the Medal of Honor for his heroic actions in the battle of Little Round Top, Colonel Chamberlain demonstrated great leadership before the first bayonet was fixed and the first shot was fired. The pivotal moment occurred when he reminded the 120 mutineers of the nobility of their cause. This quiet and unassuming colonel possessed the authority to deal harshly with these mutineers, but his earnest appeal persuaded these men to reenlist voluntarily in the heroic effort.[4] They yielded their frustrations and longings to go home and instead joined up with the Twentieth Maine Regiment. The additional numbers of these experienced troops made the difference in maintaining the left flank of the Union Army at Little Round Top. Each soldier rallied to the cause and collectively stood shoulder-to-shoulder against insurmountable odds. Many paid the ultimate price.

Why did the mutineers change their minds and do what they had firmly vowed not to do? Chamberlain intuitively understood that he could not *command* the level of commitment needed to endure the sacrifices these men would be called to make. He told them that even though he had the authority to confine or even execute them, he would not. Their re-enlistment must be voluntary. Chamberlain's appeal was effective because they saw in him a unique intermingling of authenticity, humility, self-discipline, and courage.

Because of these attributes and the resulting trust the mutineers felt for him, Chamberlain rekindled their conviction about the purpose for which they were fighting. Chamberlain's impact was tied directly to the soldiers' response to who he was as a person.

He inspired the men to rise above their resentment of the government and their miserable circumstances, homesickness, and fear. The mutineers' hearts and minds were transformed as Chamberlain fanned the embers of a higher sense of calling and purpose.

Beyond their obvious desire to go be with their families and resume their regular lives, he knew that many cherished a desire to serve a noble purpose. Like most of us, they wanted to be a part of a group that was making a difference and to be a part of something bigger than themselves. Chamberlain's speech pointed the way for an honorable resolution, and they would never be the same again.

The Person of the Leader

Inspiring others to give themselves unreservedly to the mission is not a management technique. Effective leadership is far more personal. Followers size us up as people to see if they want to follow our leadership or simply comply with our directives.

Followers want to know that the aim toward which they move is important and meaningful. Even in the military and the corporate world, which remain organizationally hierarchical, people follow leaders with high commitment only when the leader is profoundly trustworthy and when he or she pursues a clear and compelling purpose.

Inspiring others to give themselves unreservedly to the mission is not a management technique. Effective leadership is far more personal.

OUR OWN NEED FOR MEANING

We understand this desire to make an impact because we experience this need ourselves. We want to believe our lives count for something more than fighting gridlocked freeways and making it from paycheck to paycheck. In moments of quiet reflection we ask ourselves, "Is it really possible for our lives to make a difference?" When it is not apparent that we can, we feel anguish.

Steve Jobs put our need for impact in contemporary terms. "We're here to put a dent in the universe."[5]

"We're here to put a dent in the universe."

—STEVE JOBS

Do you remember how you felt when it was announced that Steve Jobs had died? I don't know about you, but I felt sadness. We probably didn't pause to analyze how he had transformed computers, movies, music, phones, how we buy computers, packaging, and so much more. No doubt

Steve Jobs will be remembered for all that and as one of the most influential leaders of the twenty-first century; however, our collective reaction was much more emotional. We missed him.

Despite his well-documented rough edges, we knew that he loved his family, and we admired his passion for excellence. We marveled that a leader could create such an impact on the world. We admired his comeback from being fired in 1985 to bringing the company roaring back from the brink of bankruptcy in 1997. It amazed us that just over a decade later, the company became the world's most highly valued corporate asset.

Our collective grief was not about Apple the company but rather about Jobs the man. We missed him and his ability to wow us again and again. We felt regret that the world too seldom gives us someone who inspires us and models the relentless pursuit of vision. We instinctively knew that, for Jobs, making something that was beautiful and yet solved real problems was more important than profits. This buoyed our faith that work could, in fact, be meaningful.

During Jobs' time at Apple, his employees had the same everyday problems we do; however, they instinctively trusted Jobs, and the power of his purpose shifted the plane of their perspective. Jobs constantly reminded them of the noble cause of their effort, and their daily problems seemed small in comparison.

Jobs' biggest gift may have been to give us hope that we, too, can make our own dent in the universe. We may not possess the creative genius or brazen determination of Steve Jobs, but his example makes us at least consider how we could make a difference in our own sphere of influence. In those quiet moments of reflection, we long for a way to get started and make an impact in some significant way.

THE CERTAIN BARRIERS

In my many years as an organizational psychologist and management consultant, I have had the privilege of working with thousands of people in hundreds of organizations around the world. When I ask leaders about their aspirations, it is fairly common for them to acknowledge that they want more challenge, responsibility, recognition, and advancement. They seek stimulating work that they look forward to accomplishing. Many also acknowledge that *they long to make an impact with their work.* Of course, they want to move forward in their careers, to have bigger jobs, to make more money, etc.; but down deep, they really want to make a positive difference and to have their lives count for something more purposeful than simply making a living. My guess is that you are no different. You, too, want to get ahead, but you also aspire to be the kind of leader who, like Chamberlain or Jobs, inspires others to give themselves unreservedly to the organization's mission and to make a meaningful difference.

In the pursuit of making an impact, we inevitably collide with barriers. One is simply the ruts we get into in everyday life. Our lives are very daily, and the mundane obligations of paying the mortgage or getting a roof leak repaired diminish our hopes and dreams and distract us from a higher purpose. "Dailyness" can quench any noble aspirations we might be nurturing.

We sometimes anesthetize our yearning for meaning and purpose with frenetic activities or addiction to the superficial, but the feeling keeps finding its way back into our awareness. An inspiring movie, a beautiful video about the wonders of the planet, a story about someone who made a difference, or anything that shifts the plane of our perspective can fuel that hope in us.

Another barrier is that when we look around our own organization, we do not see many leaders having much of an impact. There are not many role models. We wonder why is it that those who have the most power, often have the least impact. We see many of the leaders in our organization managing a bunch of stuff—just organizing the daily rat race. Very few leaders realize their aspirations. Most finish short of the vision with which they began their careers. Instead, somewhere along the line many began working for money instead of for meaning. They sought a safe retirement instead of having a meaningful impact. Some actually went off the rails, but most were simply dead on the tracks.

A Different Ending

Great leaders who leave a powerful legacy are not somehow less vulnerable to these same barriers we face. The critical question is what makes them so different?

My purpose in writing this book is to help you overcome your barriers and to give you the tools to script an incredibly better narrative. If you read and apply the principles of this book you will realize those aspirations deep inside you to create a lasting legacy. I promise that you will make an impact—the hope of every great leader.

The person inside us (our core) determines more than anything our ability to make an impact. In the chapters ahead we will learn what our core is and how to grow and protect our core, the key to achieving that hope within us!

CHAPTER 2

THREE FACES OF A LEADER

"Leadership is a potent combination of strategy and character. But if you must be without one, be without the strategy."[1]

—U.S. GENERAL NORMAN SCHWARZKOPF,
WHO COMMANDED OPERATION DESERT STORM

In my work as an organizational psychologist, I have traveled to more than twenty countries outside the United States to work with leaders and their teams. I always make an effort to bring my wife, Anne, and our sons a souvenir from the countries I visit. Just before I left for Uruguay to work with a group, a glitzy retail store's catalogue arrived in the mail. On the front cover was a rugged-looking guy wearing a beautiful brown suede coat with sheepskin lining. The handsome model stood against a jagged mountain backdrop, and he was cool. It seemed like owning a coat like this would make me cool and maybe alter my sons' perception of my being uncool. I looked at the catalogue cover again and said to myself, "That's me."

I knew that a lot of these coats were made in South America, so I decided to look for one during my trip to Montevideo. As luck would have it, one of the team members knew of a nearby factory where I could be custom-fitted one day and get the coat the next day. When our meeting ended one afternoon, I went to the factory and was measured for a coat. I could hardly wait to get home and demonstrate to my two teenage sons that I was hip and not as completely out of it as they seemed to think. I knew that they would want me to wear this coat to their football games, and that all the other kids would wish their dads had a cool coat like mine.

After arriving home, I gave Anne a beautiful sweater and the boys some other gifts from Uruguay. I then announced that I had bought something for myself on the trip. While Anne and the boys waited in the kitchen, I went to a back hallway, donned my new coat, and walked into the kitchen with all the confidence of a fashion model on a Paris runway.

A few seconds of silence passed, and the boys convulsed with laughter for what seemed like five minutes. Jim finally yelled out, "Hey, Dad, great-looking pimp coat!" My new fashion image instantly plummeted under the withering fire of teenage ridicule. I put my new coat in a storage closet in our basement, and it has never again seen the light of day.

A LEADER'S STYLE

We all have a style that defines us. My sons thought my new coat was such a significant departure from my usual style that it was very funny. Leaders, too, have styles that define them. On some occasions fashion does become a defining characteristic of our style. Mark Zuckerberg, founder and CEO of Facebook, is notorious for wearing dark gray T-shirts and a hoodie almost every day, even when meeting with important groups of investors. His dressed-down style has been described as a mark of leadership immaturity by some analysts.[2] More often than fashion, however, we think of style as reflective of how a leader presents herself to others—her manner.

Style is one of three "faces" to a leader's behavior—style, conduct, and core (Figure 2.1).

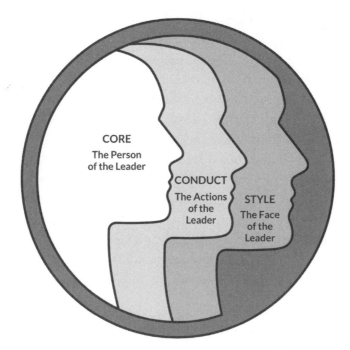

Figure 2.1

Style is the outward face of a leader. It is a leader's behavioral epidermis. Because style is the most easily observable way we interact with others, we tend to be most readily known for our style. Steve Jobs' well-documented style was abrasive and impatient.

Movies sometime accentuate the styles of various leaders to make the uniqueness of the characters more interesting. U.S. General George Patton and Mahatma Gandhi were two highly influential leaders of the twentieth century. Both men exerted huge influence on world affairs, but their outward means of expression were dramatically different. Movies about each demonstrated their unique styles. In the flag-draped opening scene of *Patton*, the general confidently swaggers to the front of the stage of a huge auditorium filled with soldiers. He is impeccably dressed in a pressed uniform, mirrored boots, riding crop, rows of medals in perfect order, and an ivory-handled revolver in a polished holster. He portrays a self-assured commander of men.

In the movie *Gandhi* we see the renowned leader address a large, angry group of men who want to take up arms against the British. Gandhi wears a modest suit, speaks in quiet tones, and urges his followers toward passive resistance in "fighting" the British. Gandhi not only helped free the Indian people from Britain, he inspired similar methods in the civil rights movement in the United States.

We see widely varying styles in corporate leaders and recognize that any number of different styles can be equally effective. One particular style may be better in a given situation. For example, Gandhi would not have been Eisenhower's choice to lead American troops against the German army in World War II. However, he was the right leader to shame the British into submission in India.

A LEADER'S CONDUCT

The second face of a leader encompasses our day-to-day actions or conduct. If our actions get good results, we are thought to be competent. Conversely, if we do not achieve the desired outcomes, we are viewed as less able.

Examples of the actions of a leader in an organization include:

- Setting a clear and compelling direction for followers.
- Building a high-performing team from those they enlist.
- Creating an engaging and productive culture.
- Responding effectively to threats and opportunities that concern a leader's vision and mission.

Skillful actions have been the topic of many books on leadership. Although books on the best practices of great leaders and the principles of good leadership have significant value, they do not get to the heart of great leadership, and they do not address the most disturbing cause of leader failure.

Most individuals seriously considered for senior leadership in an organization demonstrate an established track record documenting their competence as a leader. Their past actions and the results, good or bad, are usually readily apparent. Understandably, this résumé of performance becomes the primary basis for a hiring decision.

A Leader's Core

In working with thousands of leaders over many years, I have observed that they rarely fail because of lack of competence. Clearly competence is necessary, but it is not sufficient to be a great leader. We must also have a strong core.

The word "core" has become a major idea in the physical development of athletes and others interested in fitness. Core includes all of the muscles of the midsection. The core muscles stabilize the entire body and are prime contributors to strength and coordinated movement.[3] Athletes in just about every sport focus on developing their core muscles because it has proven to make them so much better at whatever sport they play.

Throughout this book I use the word "core" as a metaphor for the person inside us. Our core is what the ancients metaphorically referred to as our "heart" or "mind." Hebrew writers referred to core as our "inward parts." They viewed this part of us as the seat of our character, conscience, thoughts, feelings, attitudes, desires, considerations, and volition.

Our core is what the ancients metaphorically referred to as our "heart" or "mind." Hebrew writers . . . viewed this part of us as the seat of our character, conscience, thoughts, feelings, attitudes, desires, considerations, and volition.

Where is our metaphysical core located? Philosophers have debated this question over the centuries. Scientists are increasingly discovering more about the complexity and interworking of our heart, brain, and whole body in determining how we behave. Although the anatomical location of our core is ultimately not important for our purposes, Figure 2.2 graphically illustrates how we might visualize our core.

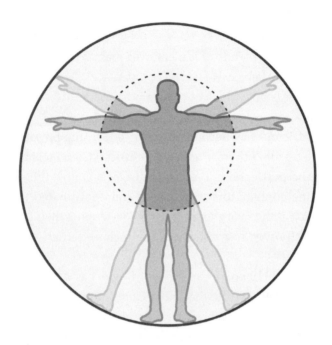

Figure 2.2

What is unarguable is that there is a "person" inside of us who is a living being. That inside person is what I am calling our core. This inner person acts, feels, thinks, speaks, has desires, makes decisions, and has identity. Our core learns, forms opinions, and is the chief repository of our beliefs. Those beliefs are formed in a number of different ways. For a leader to be effective, his or her beliefs must be intentional, not accidental. Our beliefs are a major governing factor in our behavior, and when our beliefs are sound and true, they make us better leaders—much better. When those beliefs are errant, the results can be catastrophic.

Our core has a voice, which social scientists sometimes call "self-talk." Whether we are aware of it, there is a fairly steady conversation going on inside us, and when we learn to pay attention to that voice, the revelations about ourselves can be informative if not startling. Our core's voice guides us to the beliefs we hold. Chapter 9 explores this topic in more detail.

This book is mainly about how to strengthen our core. A strong core depends upon self-awareness. It vets our beliefs and alerts us to rationalization. It controls errant impulses. It makes us authentic and emotionally resilient. A strong core prevents us from going down that path of personal destruction that many have taken.

LEADING FROM INSIDE

Truly engaging others flows from the essence of who we are—from our core. When we have a strong core, people trust us and follow us with abandon. Management is positional; leadership is personal. Colonel Chamberlain possessed the position from which to manage his men, but he chose to lead them instead. I believe they accepted Chamberlain's leadership because he appealed to them from deep within the core of who he was and spoke to the core of each man in the disgruntled regiment. The leader's core connected to the mutineer's core, and they followed.

> *Management is positional;*
> *leadership is personal.*

Intentionally engaging the heart and soul of followers today is not a part of a typical leader's modus operandi. Many take the expected path of expediency and pragmatism—they focus on getting the job done. The challenge of great leadership is not only to ensure that the daily transactions are completed well, but also to garner the commitment of followers so that they willingly exceed the basic requirements of their jobs.

A strong personal core grants a leader access to that same deep place in others, and it can reach the place where a follower's voluntary commitment originates. When our core appears strong to others, they trust us. Trust is not the end state, but it does cause a follower to open the window to his core. When the leader's core reaches the follower's core, a far deeper level of commitment to the mission occurs just as we saw with Chamberlain's mutineers.

The access we gain to another's core gives us power to influence that person far beyond simple compliance. Influence comes from the Latin word, *influere*, which means "to flow into." It reflects the power to produce an effect without force or command . . . the action of producing a result on the actions, behavior, and opinions of another. Others will only trust us enough for our ideas, opinions, and feelings to "flow into them" if they believe in the soundness of our core. Like the mutineers, our followers need to sense that our core is sound, which then makes our influence effective. Chamberlain spoke from his core to connect with his soldiers' deep need to find meaning in their own lives.

---

*The access we gain to another's core
gives us power to influence that person
far beyond simple compliance.*

Chamberlain had great impact on the battlefield (and on the United States) because he engaged the hearts and minds of a group of disillusioned soldiers. His strong foundation—his core—made it possible for him to speak to his followers' cores and elevate their perspective to the noble purpose of continuing to fight. The mutineers set aside their disaffection, because the unshakable personal foundation of Chamberlain's core inspired them.

When we look at effective leaders today, inevitably they have a strong core. Conversely, my research demonstrates that those who fall from leadership have almost always suffered a compromised core.

Enduring Leadership Starts with a Strong Core

The short tenure of many senior leaders makes it clear that effective leadership is very hard to sustain. The conditions under which people lose their position and influence teach us a lot about how to preserve it. A critical discovery is that falling from a leadership position often has very little to do with a leader's competence but has *everything* to do with his or her core.[4]

David Petraeus, a former four-star general and head of the CIA, was forced to resign because of an extramarital affair with his biographer, Paula Broadwell. He did not resign because of a brusque military style or because the president was disappointed with his accomplishments in the military or at the CIA. Petraeus, like many other leaders who get off track, experienced a breach of his core. The U.S. president accepted Petraeus's resignation because he knew it would be impossible for Petraeus to continue his service without compromise and distraction. The reputation of any leader is far more fragile than we think, and the consequences of a seriously dysfunctional core almost always make a leader's continuance in his or her present role impossible.

Our core is the *foundation* from which we lead. When our foundation is trustworthy, we possess the potential to profoundly elicit greatness in others. When our foundation is weak, we lose the platform from which we lead. If we could interview the engineers of the Tower of Pisa, their lessons-learned list would undoubtedly start off with "Foundations matter."

While our style and conduct are much more visible, our core is deeper and less easily observable and accessible. All three faces of leadership play critical roles in our effectiveness; however, it is our core that plays the most impactful role in making us strong leaders able to exercise great influence over followers. A strong core ultimately trumps style and competence in sustaining our ability to lead.

A strong core ultimately trumps style and competence in sustaining our ability to lead.

When our core is intact and congruent, others experience us as authentic, humble, and trustworthy. When our core is compromised or conflicted, others experience us as arrogant, self-serving, and insecure. No matter how artful their style or competent their actions, every failed leader I have studied had a malfunctioning core—it had been broken in some significant way.

CRACKS IN THE CORE ARE HARD TO SEE

Why do some leaders who have cracks in their foundation rise to the top? Part of the dilemma is that some aspects of what determine whether a leader will perform well are far less visible than stellar achievements. A board member of a company recently pointed out to me that their last two CEOs failed. One was incredibly arrogant, and no one bought into his vision. The other had an affair with a senior officer, which became very public, totally undermining both their credibility. As we talked about my research on the causes of derailment, the board member literally threw his hands up in the air with visible exasperation and said, "We're good at screening our CEO candidates for competence but we're lousy at screening them for what goes on inside them. If we don't get this right this time, we're doomed!"

Because of the two consecutive flawed CEOs, what the board member really wanted was to find some way to vet a CEO candidate's core—his or her inner person. Many in a position to select a senior leader simply do not know how to do this. This type of imaging technology does not exist—there's no MRI for our core!

I have actually seen management overlook a worker's faulty core because of his or her stellar competence and job performance. Individuals who achieved significant results were catapulted into senior management positions. When they eventually failed cataclysmically, the failure was not rooted in a lack of competence, but rather in a chronically compromised core. The stress of a much bigger job simply revealed more glaringly what was there all along. It always seemed to me that, had that person's manager, a mentor, or even a peer paid closer attention or been willing to confront a given individual's core problems earlier in their career, a different narrative might have been written.

It may be that a younger leader's core starts out strong, but as he or she grows in responsibility and influence, power begins to chip away the foundation. As we will see in Chapter 6, when leaders rise in responsibility and influence, we often see the pernicious effect of power on their core. Many leaders earlier in their careers were good people with good intentions, but something happened on the way to the top. Unregulated power is one of the chief instigators of a compromised core.

WE MUST BUILD ON A SOUND CORE

As we have seen, the foundation of great leadership is our core. To be a leader who has great impact, we must build and protect a strong core. There are a number of disciplines in the upcoming chapters that help us in this endeavor. When effectively exercised, these disciplines keep our core strong, help us have great influence over others, and put us in a position to have huge impact as leaders. The practice of these disciplines is vital. Without diligence and intentionality we cannot protect and grow our core, and our ability to make an impact will be fleeting and temporary.

My guess is that on two subjects we are in absolute agreement. First, we want to optimize our effectiveness in leading others such that they truly give themselves unreservedly to the mission. Second, we want to steer ourselves clear of that terrible path of personal destruction that so many leaders seem to follow. Both are tied to an intact core.

To have the impact we seek, we must understand our core and how it functions and then use these insights to transform our behavior. It requires courage to look deep inside ourselves and, if needed, to forcefully change what we find.

CHAPTER 3

WE ARE OUR OWN BLACK BOX

*"As a face is reflected in water
so the heart reflects the real person."*[1]

—ANCIENT PROVERB

A few years ago, my wife, Anne, and I attended a conference at a beautiful island resort to hear a number of well-known speakers. The foundation that sponsored the event sought to inform the attendees about various charitable needs around the world. One of the speakers known for his great sense of humor and ability to tell stories thanked the foundation board profusely for inviting him to speak at the meeting and for taking us all to such a nice place. He went on for several minutes about how beautiful the setting was and how rarely he was a guest in this type of resort. In an effort to be humorously self-deprecating, the speaker said that he usually stayed in budget hotels and named one hotel chain in particular. He then said, "You know the first thing I have to do when I stay in that hotel is to go into my room and kill all the roaches." Off to our left there was a loud gasp and a wave of disturbance in the audience, almost as if someone was having a medical emergency. Unbeknownst to the speaker, the family of the deceased founder of the just-mentioned hotel chain was in the audience! The family and their close friends sitting nearby recoiled at the speaker's astoundingly insensitive attempt at humor, and the unsettled feeling in the broader audience became palpable.

The following morning, the speaker asked the sponsors if he could talk with the group again. As he stood at the podium, this greatly admired speaker humbly apologized to the family and to the audience for his remarks the afternoon before. He acknowledged that this occurrence galvanized his attention. He had spent much of the previous night looking at himself and asking how this could have happened. Then, in an amazing display of openness and vulnerability, he shared about his own struggle with needing approval—something that had been largely absent in his growing-up years. He became very effective at engineering the approval he sought, and humor was his number one tool—make people laugh, and they will like you. He confessed that he resisted acknowledging this dark side of himself and had never discussed it with anyone else. In the middle of the night, he vowed that his offense to the family the afternoon before would break the cycle. His authenticity was profoundly moving as he and others in the audience wept. The family accepted his apology with grace and forgiveness. His transparency was amazingly redemptive and helped rekindle the emotional lift among the participants that the sponsors hoped to achieve.

DID I REALLY SAY THAT?

Why do regrettable comments leap from our own lips? We all say and do dumb things, and very many times simply do not know "what got into us." Those actions for which we would love a do-over or the words we wish we could reel back wake us in the middle of the night. We are particularly troubled when our reputation is diminished or when others are hurt by our words or actions.

More important, how do we ensure that our words and actions create the desired effect—having a positive influence on others? How do we inspire and engage others to give their highest and best effort to the cause at hand?

As discussed in the last chapter, we grow and protect our core through the practice of several disciplines. The first is self-examination, in which we intentionally scrutinize our thoughts, feelings, attitudes, habits, and the factors that influence them. We use this discipline to discover that person inside us who thinks, feels, believes, and forms self-authored opinions. The goal is to become an authority on who we are.

It is a discipline that requires focus. My wife, Anne, takes Pilates from an instructor who tells her that exercise requires as much mental focus as physical. She has to move certain muscles while breathing a particular way. Understanding and managing our core is much the same.

The intended result of self-examination is self-awareness, which then opens the door to self-regulation. If we become aware of a thought or feeling that might lead us astray, self-regulation reins in errant impulses, like making a regrettable statement. Self-examination is the introspective discipline that leads to self-awareness. We can then use that awareness to guide our actions.

A very savvy CEO with whom I worked for a number of years told me that a particular regional field director really "pulled his chain." When I asked him to elaborate, he acknowledged that this particular sales guy was very successful and had a huge ego. He constantly complained and pontificated about what he saw as poor service at the home office. Sometimes, he aimed his criticism at the CEO personally. Before any conversation with this particular field rep, the CEO would go through a mental self-awareness exercise so that he stayed "grounded" during his interactions. In the heat of conflict with the field rep, he wanted to keep his wits and not overreact to his criticism. Most of the time it worked, and he was able to have a civil conversation and focus on solving the problem.

Effective self-regulation is dependent upon and highly interactive with self-examination and self-awareness, as shown in Figure 3.1 (see next page).

The purpose of this chapter is to demonstrate the importance of self-examination and how this discipline makes self-awareness and self-regulation possible. Skillful self-examination builds a strong core, which makes us more effective leaders.

Figure 3.1

I don't know about you, but I tend to be a bit uncomfortable with "navel gazing." A friend told me the other day that introspection feels like she's giving herself a colonoscopy. Self-examination is not a natural tendency for most of us, and, candidly, not my first impulse for how to spend time away from work. I am frequently drawn to the superficial and feel pretty much like the couple in this *New Yorker* cartoon (see following page).

We resist looking deep into ourselves for a variety of reasons—maybe it has never occurred to us to even look in the first place or maybe there are some demons in there we do not want to face. We may not even know how to look. Maybe the payoff for making the effort is not that apparent. We might also worry that if we look deep down, there may not be much of a deep down. One friend of mine describes himself as a "shallow coper" and prefers not to deal with his core. Many avoid seeking to examine and understand themselves, and our culture makes it easy to operate at a surface level.

During the beginning stages of a consulting assignment, I frequently interview members of the leadership team. Certain impressions form very quickly. Is the person direct, authentic, and perceptive about themselves? Does the person possess keen insight into other team members? Occasionally, I have a distinct sense that a person is not particularly self-aware. During a recent interview, I wrote a note in the margin, "Stranger to himself." This is always a self-limiting liability.

Intentional self-examination is a critical step on the path to great leadership. It is like a tool in the hands of a skilled craftsman. Careful use of this tool lays the groundwork for self-regulation that can prevent us from blunting our effectiveness and falling short of the impact we desire.

Our core functions like the black box in airplanes. Just as investigators use the box for their analysis of what went wrong if a plane veers off course or crashes, effective leaders can look to their core for a more accurate understanding of themselves. To achieve the impact for which we strive, we must seek to understand and harness the unique forces that will make us more effective as well as to diminish those weaknesses that will render us less so. This discipline requires deliberate and relentless effort.

SEEING WITH THE EYES OF OUR CORE

Self-examination is about seeing with the "eyes of our core." The eyes in our head see the physical world around us. The eyes of our core provide *insight* about our beliefs, thoughts, feelings, motives, and actions. Leaders who create an impact use these types of insights to become more effective. Their elevated level of self-awareness is forged in the furnace of self-examination.

Their elevated level of self-awareness is forged in the furnace of self-examination.

Seeing with our core falls into three categories:

1. Past—looking at our behavior after the fact (retrospective).
2. Future—being thoughtful in advance (prospective).
3. Present—analyzing what is occurring in the here and now (contemporaneous).

LOOKING BACKWARD

Self-examination of the past involves looking at specific events that already took place—think of it as looking in the rearview mirror. After his blunder, the "roach killer" might have asked himself some questions, such as, "Why did I feel such a need to flatter the sponsors of the meeting? Am I trying to get them to like me and invite me back? Why did I feel a need to tell that story? What kept me from seeing the obviously offensive nature of that story? How did my need for approval cloud my judgment? What can I do differently next time to assure that never happens again?"

In a much broader context, retrospective self-reflection also seeks to understand the life experiences that influence our behavior. If we wish to lead skillfully, we must consider the forces that have made us who we are.

Background Influences

- our parents' background, such as their education, occupation, income, social standing, and religious heritage
- where we grew up
- our education
- our teachers and coaches
- our friends and peer group
- what we read
- what we see and hear in media
- the places we have lived and visited
- the leaders and mentors we have had
- the organizations for which we have worked
- our colleagues
- and the groups to which we have belonged

The above is a list of extraordinarily complex, interwoven forces that contribute to who we are—no wonder we are so complex and hard to figure out! Pick just one from the list to see how profoundly these forces have guided your life. For example, what if you had gone to a different school? How would you be different today? At the end of this chapter I will recommend an exercise to further understand how these forces have influenced you.

Our backgrounds help define us, but they do not have to limit us or dictate our future. Some in our society have a "victim" mentality and believe they are held captive to their backgrounds. I do not believe this. There are many examples of people who escaped from the worst imaginable circumstances. These forces do not exert absolute control over us; however, they inevitably do shape our beliefs, values, personality, interests, and abilities. This is why it is important to reflect on where we have been. The involved process of understanding our backgrounds is like peeling an onion and continues over our lifetime. Intentional self-examination leads to thoughtful, deliberate choices about who I am and how I am going to be on an ongoing basis.

If we intend to be a person of disproportionate influence, we must study ourselves to understand these many factors so that nothing in our background unduly influences us. We can "re-decide" who we are going to be and choose to break the power of even enduring habits.

I met a very influential woman not long ago who was born into poverty, but she decided not to be a victim of her circumstances. Amazingly, she had the presence of mind as a young girl to notice people in society who were successful. She actually had a conversation with herself and said, "I can be one of those people." One of the keys was that she decided to become an excellent student and then asserted her way into some of the finest schools in the United States. She is now a highly visible leader who has an impact on thousands of people. She is truly a remarkable person, but she would argue that anyone with self-awareness and determination can overcome their circumstances.

LOOKING AHEAD

Self-examination about opportunities before us is profoundly important. Thinking in advance about an upcoming interaction or event and reflecting on how our strengths and weaknesses may influence the outcome is a much better option than trying to dig out of a hole created by a careless act or word. If the conference speaker mentioned earlier had a private conversation with himself before he spoke to our group the first time, I believe he would have experienced a very different result and not clouded the very important message he came to deliver. His inner conversation might have gone like this:

> I'm really looking forward to speaking to this group in this beautiful resort. It was a privilege to be invited. . . . Be genuinely apprecia-tive. I don't have to fawn all over the sponsors trying to get them to like me. I also need to be especially careful about stories and jokes with this group, because I really don't know who is in the audience. Stay away from comments that might unintentionally offend this audience that has very high ideals about making a global impact. Focus on the extraordinary opportunities that are before them to consider.

What I am about to propose is not easy given the normal demands on a leader's time, but this practice can be life-changing. Begin and end your workday with a brief period of reflection. Taking fifteen minutes at the beginning of the day can help us stay on track throughout the day. Ask yourself if there is anything that might compromise your effectiveness today (e.g., fatigue, lack of courage, irritation with a fellow executive, etc.). Simply knowing about these factors may help you mitigate their influence. We should also take a few minutes at the end of the day to inventory how we did at implementing our resolutions.

What I am about to propose is not easy given the normal demands on a leader's time, but this practice can be life-changing. Begin and end your workday with a brief period of reflection.

Occasionally take a longer period to more thoughtfully dissect some of the factors from the Background Influences list. Try to understand how those factors have influenced your behavior. As in the example of the influential woman above, there may be influences from your background that you want to rethink. I know a woman whose parents gave her a "cute" name. They probably felt warm and cuddly about their new little baby, but they did not think about the liability her somewhat silly name would become when she tried to establish herself as credible adult in the workplace at thirty years old. When she moved to a new job, she decided to legally change her name to be taken more seriously. She told me that her parents still call her by the cute name. I am not suggesting that you change your name, but you might use the Background Influences list as a guide to consider what aspects of your background could be hindering you in some significant way.

LOOKING SIDE-TO-SIDE

The third type of self-examination, being thoughtful in the here and now, is a more advanced skill. It requires that we monitor our feelings and intuitions as they occur. With this skill we are often able to adjust our behavior in the present. When someone criticizes my idea, my first impulse may be to bristle. We can use that "bristling feeling" as a mental prompt or early-warning system. For example, we might say to ourselves, "This is a self-awareness moment. I need to rein in that impulse and not get defensive. Responding to this person in the way I am inclined at present is not going help anybody. I need to sit on my response for a while until I am not responding emotionally."

Self-examination in the here and now is not easy, because it requires our brains to multitask. We have to pay attention to the content of whatever we are doing, while at the same time, monitoring and adjusting our emotional responses and actions in the present. For example, I could find myself in a meeting, discussing how we are going to respond to a customer complaint. I also may be brimming with resentment about how Susan just threw my brilliant idea under the beer truck. Maybe I need to speak to myself and say, "I have to stay engaged with the topic without letting Susan's barb get me off task."

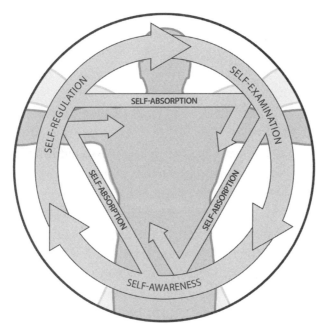

Figure 3.2

THE GRAVITATIONAL FORCE
OF YOURSELF

All this self-examination might seem like a bit much. It is important that we not mistake self-examination for self-absorption. As Figure 3.2 illustrates, self-absorption is a departure from healthy self-examination.

One of my professors in grad school used to say, "The first time you look in the mirror is for yourself. The second time you look in the mirror is for others. The third time you look . . . well, you're in trouble!" We need to look in the mirror and use the information to affirm our strengths or transform a weakness but not to become preoccupied with ourselves. Healthy self-examination is very different from the narcissism inherent in self-absorption. A self-absorbed person views self-reflection as an end in itself, which is nothing more than a preoccupation with his or her own inner workings. These are the people who actually enjoy navel gazing!

DON'T ALWAYS TRY THIS ALONE

Much of what we have considered up until now rests upon our willingness to journey privately through healthy self-examination. It is crucial to point out that self-reflection sometimes ensues from "internal processing" and at other times through "external processing." Internal processing occurs when we reflect privately. External processing involves self-discovery through others. Ideally, we do both; however, if we are "extroverted," we may find self-reflection easier when we involve others. Expressing thoughts helps extroverts to form and to evaluate an idea, so having a sounding board is vital. Self-disclosure and self-discovery work in tandem to make extroverts more aware.

Introverts, on the other hand, do their best processing through private self-reflection, but it is critical that they validate their private insights by testing them with others. Although an introvert's personal reflection may be accurate, he or she should make sure that objective friends or colleagues validate their perceptions. Conversely, I recommend to extroverts that they also learn how to reflect alone. Incidentally, if you are not certain about whether you gravitate more toward external processing or internal processing, just type extroversion/introversion into a search engine and you will get an abundance of information.

Thoughtful and intentional self-examination is a critical discipline that is not only enlightening, but also transformational. Developing self-knowledge is a journey into unchartered territory for many; however, it is a discipline that's critical for guarding your core and becoming the kind of leader who makes an impact. We will look at a number of other disciplines that guard our core but intentional self-examination is the beginning point.

GO DEEPER

As I mentioned earlier, it is helpful to begin and end every day with a short period of reflection. On occasion (several times a year), it may be helpful to carve out a longer time to do a deeper dive.

Self-Awareness Survey

The following self-scoring survey assesses your attitudes about self-reflection. Place a check mark in the box ranging from 1 to 5 to rate where you are on the various items.

1. I examine my thoughts, feelings, actions on a consistent basis:

1	2	3	4	5
Not at All Descriptive		Sometimes Descriptive		Highly Descriptive

2. I am intentional and work hard to find meaning in my work:

1	2	3	4	5
Not at All Descriptive		Sometimes Descriptive		Highly Descriptive

3. I am consciously aware of how the background factors listed on page 27 have influenced who I am today, and I know which of those factors I must consciously work on to diminish their impact:

1	2	3	4	5
Not at All Descriptive		Sometimes Descriptive		Highly Descriptive

4. I keep a journal about what happens at work and reflect on what did and did not go well, and my role and responsibility in each case. I ask myself what I could have done differently. When an interaction or other event goes badly, I seize it as a learning opportunity. I take personal responsibility for poor outcomes and resolve how I will handle similar events differently.

1	2	3	4	5
Not at All Descriptive		Sometimes Descriptive		Highly Descriptive

5. When I learn that I have misunderstood an important message sent by someone, I look for ways to improve my hearing.

1	2	3	4	5
Not at All Descriptive		Sometimes Descriptive		Highly Descriptive

6. I discuss any recurring challenges at work with a trusted advisor and ask him or her to help me better understand my role in those challenges and the appropriate response.

1	2	3	4	5
Not at All Descriptive		Sometimes Descriptive		Highly Descriptive

7. I routinely reflect on how my strengths and weaknesses may foster or hinder what I need to get done today.

1	2	3	4	5
Not at All Descriptive		Sometimes Descriptive		Highly Descriptive

8. I reflect on whose cooperation I need to achieve my goals. I carefully consider where the "trip wires" in those relationships may be so that I carefully avoid them.

1	2	3	4	5
Not at All Descriptive		Sometimes Descriptive		Highly Descriptive

9. I make a point to attribute positive motives to those with whom I disagree.

1	2	3	4	5
Not at All Descriptive		Sometimes Descriptive		Highly Descriptive

10. I use self-awareness tools (such as like the Myers-Briggs Type Indicator and the DISC Profile System*) to help me be more conscious of my own "internal wiring" and general predispositions.

1	2	3	4	5
Not at All Descriptive		Sometimes Descriptive		Highly Descriptive

1. Add your scores on the ten items.

2. Calibrate how you did on the following ranges:

46–50 Outstanding—hall of fame material

36–45 Good

26–35 OK but needs some work

20–25 Get busy and make this better

<20 Needs some serious in-depth attention

3. Create an action plan as to how you will strengthen your self-examination.

☐ Identify two or three actions you will begin to implement this important discipline.

☐ Determine when you will start.

☐ Determine how can you be accountable to someone to make this discipline a habit.

---

* Simple versions of the Myers-Briggs are available online or go to the Center for the Application of Psychological Type: www.capt.org. Google your four letters and learn about your type. Particularly look for information about how your type acts under stress. The DISC Profile System is available at Triaxia Partners (http://www.teamresources.com/category/site-location/disc-profile-system%C2%AE-customized-application-reports).

As we discussed earlier in this chapter (Figure 3.1), the real aim of self-examination is self-awareness, which makes self-regulation possible. We need a bridge from self-examination to self-awareness. In the chapter that follows, we will build that bridge.

CHAPTER 4

KNOW THYSELF

"Knowing what is right is like deep water in the heart;
a wise person draws from the well within."[1]

—ANCIENT PROVERB

A close friend of mine is a business school professor who uses innova-
tive learning techniques such as simulations to teach students about
the realities of corporate life. One afternoon his students formed two
teams and negotiated a mock business deal. One team decided to disad-
vantage the other team by misleading them about what they would do if
the other team made some concessions on the terms of the deal. They sold
the new terms under the guise that everyone achieved a better deal. When
it became clear that the deceptive team violated the trust of the other, one
member of the losing team stormed out of the classroom. Later he showed
up at my friend's office to talk about the experience. This particular student
had recently left the military. The company he commanded had suffered
heavy casualties during a particularly intense period of fighting. For him,
trust in one another is tantamount to survival. Having his trust violated
so cavalierly by his classmates was extremely stressful for him, and the
exercise brought forward the intense effect of his background issues.

The good news is that it became a teachable moment for the young
soldier. As my friend sat with the student in his office, he reasoned with
him about his intense feelings about the classroom simulation. The soldier
acknowledged that he had almost died because a fellow officer in another

company had not kept his commitment to provide reinforcements by a certain time. When his business school classmate reneged on his agreement, he had flashbacks about the vulnerability he felt that day when he lost five members of his company. He ran from the classroom to escape the images and sounds of explosions going off in his head. Although not pleased that his classmate had lied to him, he agreed that he overreacted to the classroom exercise. The young soldier then had a self-awareness breakthrough. "I came back to school too soon after being discharged from the Marines. I needed to take more time to get over my deployments and to discover a new normal."

My friend helped this young veteran withdraw from school and suggested some avenues for help re-entering civilian life before continuing his studies. Fortunately, the soldier received some excellent help and re-enrolled in school a year later much better integrated personally and socially and more self-aware.

After his discussion with the soldier, my friend also instigated a self-awareness moment for the leader of the deceptive team. In a private coaching session, he asked the young MBA student why he thought deception was an acceptable negotiating approach. He pointed out that he would last about five minutes in a real business context if he ever tried to mislead someone to gain competitive advantage. He did not tell him the full impact his behavior had on his classmate.

Although we may not have experienced the intense combat as my friend's student had, our unique experiences can powerfully influence who we are, what we believe, and how we act, so we must understand their impact. Knowing about and managing these forces is nonnegotiable if we want to guard our core and be a leader who thrives.

SELF-EXAMINATION LEADS TO SELF-AWARENESS

Recently I had my annual medical exam. The test results and in-office exam indicated that several aspects of my physical health needed attention. My physician prescribed several remedies to improve my health. The medical exam gave me a new awareness, but ultimately it is up to me to act on my awareness to actually benefit. It is crucial to form new habits, and this requires self-regulation, the topic of an upcoming chapter.

In the previous chapter we discussed the critical importance of intentional self-examination. My research demonstrates that healthy self-awareness is a common denominator among leaders who forge a great legacy, so the purpose of this chapter is to describe how we can become more self-aware.

Accurate self-awareness is an essential element of great leadership and personal effectiveness. When we understand our strengths and our vulnerabilities, we are better able to deploy our strengths toward the challenges of our role. We also minimize our weaknesses so that we do not undermine our relationships or otherwise blunt the efficacy of important initiatives.

GROW OUR SELF-AWARENESS

Figure 4 on the following page illustrates the idea that we grow our self-awareness through enlarging the open window.[2]

The left side of the circle comprises our "open self," which reflects a general awareness about who we are. This is an open or fully transparent "window" through which we see ourselves clearly. Others clearly see who we are as well. There is no "curtain" blocking our view of ourselves, as there is in front of the blind and hidden windows. A person who wants greater self-awareness is constantly seeking ways to enlarge this window and draws the curtain to the right. As we grow in self-awareness, we enlarge our open window while simultaneously diminishing the blind and the hidden areas.

One critical by-product of a larger open window is personal authenticity. Today, perhaps more than ever, personal authenticity is needed to lead effectively. Authenticity depends heavily on self-awareness and then on our willingness to disclose who we are—to make our open window transparent to others. Followers want to know who their leaders are, and this knowledge forms a basis for trust. Conversely, when our open area is small, others sense a lack of authenticity with a resulting diminishment of trust.

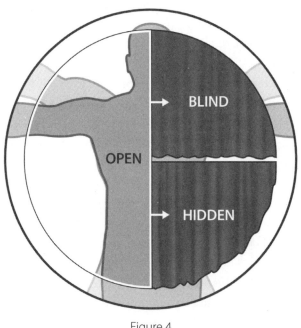

Figure 4

Authentic leaders express a
personal narrative alongside their vision
and goals for the organization.

When I am asked to evaluate a candidate for a leadership role, I look at the depth and quality of his or her self-disclosure, which is a major indicator of good self-awareness. An important distinction is that good self-disclosure is not just talking about oneself. Rather it is the revealing of insight about how to best deploy one's strengths and mitigate weaknesses. There is a tone of, "I know myself and am able to use that information for the good of my team and the organization."

In my experience, the best leaders express a personal narrative alongside their vision and goals for the organization. Both are needed for the leader to be trusted. A personal narrative flows from our background, our beliefs, our values, and our personal insights—all products of a large open window. Recently, I observed a new senior leader introduce himself to the organization he was hired to lead. There had been some quiet rumbling because he was not planning to move his family to the company's home office location. As he talked about his hopes for the organization, he took the issue head on. "I know that many of you have questions about my not moving my family to Texas. I respect and understand your concerns. My wife and I discussed this challenge at length and decided that we wanted our third child to finish high school where he attends now. He's been the kid who never sunk down any roots over my corporate career. We decided that keeping him in a school where he's finally made some good friends and done well academically and at lacrosse was worth some sacrifice on our part. I want you to know that I've unpacked my emotional bags here and am fully vested in my role for the long term. I'll commute on weekends, and when our son graduates, my wife and I look forward to her joining me here. Thank you for understanding this personal decision." During these comments a photo of the new leader with his arm around his smiling sixteen-year-old son in a lacrosse uniform appeared on the screen. The rumbling stopped, and the consensus was, "We like this guy. He's for real." Because he was he so open in his self-disclosure, employees experienced him as authentic. The company has prospered under his leadership.

BLIND SPOTS

I am always startled when the lane next to me on the freeway looks clear in my car's side-view mirror, but when I turn to double check, I see a car beside me. As broad as my mirror's coverage might be, there are blind spots. In a similar fashion, we have personal blind spots that, unheeded, can wreck us.

Some blind spots are inconsequential. I was in a hurry after being in a particularly pokey airport security line recently and missed a belt loop as I hurried to get my shoes, belt, and coat back on after exiting the line. Someone later told me about the missed belt loop. I thanked the person, but candidly, no alarm bells went off—I may not have looked like a Ralph Lauren ad, but my pants were in no danger of falling down.

Other blind spots are far more consequential. I had an assignment to meet with an executive to tell him that people had reacted very badly to the speech he gave at an awards banquet during their annual management conference. He was completely flummoxed. He certainly meant well as he tried to support company values, but most of the audience perceived him as negative and critical of their work. The reaction to his speech revealed a blind spot of considerable importance. He benefited significantly from knowing that his self-perceptions were seriously out of step with how others experienced him. Over a short period of time, he made great progress in his ability to communicate more effectively. This experience helped this leader better understand the old truism, "We judge ourselves by our intentions, while others judge us by our behavior."

We judge ourselves by our intentions,
while others judge us by our behavior.

THE CRITICAL IMPORTANCE OF FEEDBACK

To paraphrase the Scottish poet Robert Burns, "Oh that God would give us the gift to see ourselves as others do." In Figure 4, the upper right part of the circle (Blind) describes what others see in our behavior that we do not. A curtain blocking our self-awareness is drawn in front. Because we cannot see some aspects of our behavior, it is vital that we know how to enlighten ourselves on a practical level. Feedback from others is the most powerful means of opening up our blind area. Feedback takes space from the blind area and enlarges the open area. It pushes the curtain to the right. As we discussed earlier, openness in a leader is a great asset, so we must develop a hunger for feedback and seek out opportunities to receive it.

When my dad was a commercial pilot, the last ten years of his career he flew from Atlanta to Europe three to four times a month. Even back in the 1980s, the navigation equipment was fairly sophisticated. He could take off from Atlanta and turn the plane over to the computer-based auto-pilot. The plane would fly itself to the right country, the right city, and the right airport, and even land itself unassisted on the right runway. In the middle of the night during his watch, he would often see the plane's wheel turn itself to the left, gently banking the plane. The jet stream blew the plane off course fairly frequently, and the geostationary satellite provided feedback to the autopilot to get the plane back on course. My dad said it was like a ghost was flying the airplane. Thousands of pilots who fly every month entrust their very lives, and those under their care, to these geostationary satellites, confident that they provide accurate feedback to the cockpit of the plane in which they are flying.

Our blind area puts us in potential peril. We need others in our lives who function as those satellites to let us know when we are off course. Receiving personal feedback diminishes the blind area and is vital to keep us on course. Feedback pushes the curtain to the right (Figure 4) and enlarges our open area.

To pull back the curtain on our blind areas, it is essential that we have people who will speak to us with uncensored openness and directness. Spouses can be especially good at cutting to the chase. A man was driving home from attending a gala during which he received a prestigious leadership award. He mused with his wife about the evening and asked, "I wonder how many truly great men there are in the world today?" Her response: "Well there's one less than you think."

Leaders need to open channels that ensure they are receiving frequent and constructive feedback. When receiving feedback, value other's opinions even when you disagree. Be teachable. Here are several ideas:

- Develop a group of trusted advisors who will regularly give you competent and candid feedback. When I served in a leadership role of a large company, I had individuals whose insights about me and my role were tremendously helpful. I met with these advisors every month or two individually and occasionally as a group.
- Be especially receptive to feedback from people who are below you on the organization chart. As the recipients of your leadership these members often have great insight.
- Create a culture in your sphere of influence where feedback is valued, expected, and normative. Mistakes and failures are to be milked for everything they are worth.

Hidden Compromises Really Matter

A tiny, almost imperceptible flaw led to great drama in the nearly catastrophic flight of United Air 232 from Denver to Chicago on July 19, 1989. The fan disk in the DC-10's rear engine exploded, severing all three hydraulic lines, a highly improbable event—a billion-to-one chance. An investigation later discovered that the titanium ingot used to manufacture the fan disk had a tiny imperfection that had weakened to the breaking point. It took eighteen years and 15,503 takeoffs and landings to discover the problem. A jumbo jet with no hydraulics at 37,000 feet all but guaranteed a horrendous death for the 300 people on board, simply because a microscopically small bubble of nitrogen had not completely dissolved in the titanium ingot. The bubble was the tiny cause of a huge effect. Because of the crew's extraordinary skill and heroic efforts, the aircraft was able to land, and 188 of the 300 passengers survived.

Flaws in our core are like that small nitrogen bubble. They may not show up for a long time, but the mounting pressures of business find that point of imperfection. Over the course of time, a metaphorical nitrogen bubble does its work eroding the integrity of our personal core. While a blind spot is something others see that we do not, a hidden area is something no one sees without intentional effort. Often hidden aspects of our core impose themselves on our conscious awareness and are revealed forcefully and unexpectedly. This is one reason self-examination and self-awareness are so important. We need to look at ourselves carefully to find those nitrogen bubbles that often show up at the worst possible times.

A LEADER'S NITROGEN BUBBLE

A recent public example is Anthony Weiner, an influential U.S. congressman from New York and touted as a promising candidate for mayor of New York City. He resigned from Congress in disgrace after sending a lewd photo to a college student over the Internet. Weiner said at a news conference announcing his resignation,

> This was a very dumb thing to do, and it was a destructive thing to do. But it wasn't part of any plan to be hurtful to my wife. It wasn't part of a plan to be deceitful to you. It wasn't part of a plan to be—it wasn't part of a plan. It was a destructive thing that I did that I accept responsibility for. But if you're—*if you're looking for some kind of deep explanation for it, I simply don't have one except that I'm sorry.* (Italics are mine for emphasis.)

Weiner made it clear that he felt very disconnected from his actions. Of course he was sorry. His sordid act was plastered across page-one headlines around the globe. What he needed was the deep explanation that evaded him. We cannot know his motives, but that is why understanding the hidden or less accessible parts of our personality is important.

What was Weiner's nitrogen bubble that ultimately led to the failure of his core? Maybe he actually believed the *Cosmopolitan* magazine article lauding him as one of the "101 Gorgeous Real Life Bachelors"[3] written about him several years before he was married. Maybe his nitrogen bubble was simply the arrogance that brings so many other influential leaders down.

Weiner let his nitrogen bubble go undetected, enabling it to do its work. What if he had been more courageous and disciplined in his self-examination? What early-warning signs did he miss? How could he have been more thoughtful about the disgrace his actions would bring to his wife? What if Weiner had used his "phone-a-friend" option and said to a respected colleague, "Hey, I'm thinking about sending a photo of my genitals to a college student in Seattle I've never met . . . is that a good idea?" The simple act of testing his idea with a trusted advisor might have been all that was needed to conclude that "This is a really dumb idea." A "deeper understanding" of his hidden area was, in fact, the preventative medicine he needed. Fresh revelations revealed that Weiner continued sexting between the time he resigned from Congress and when he announced his candidacy for mayor of New York. Weiner lost all credibility and garnered barely five percent of the vote in his loss of the democratic primary.[4] It is unlikely that you are considering doing anything like what Congressman Weiner did, but we all do dumb things and make statements we wish we could reel back in. An essential aspect of protecting our core involves thoughtful introspection into the hidden, less-accessible forces that shape our lives. This includes aspects of ourselves that we resist thinking about, much less talking about. We have to look in our hidden area to find any nitrogen bubbles. When discovered, our open area enlarges (Figure 4). We become a healthier, more self-aware person and a better leader.

A Nitrogen Bubble I Discovered in Me

We need to look for anything that might hold us back. In an organization where I worked, I did not like the CEO's executive assistant (my sense was that the feeling was mutual). This is probably the last person in an organization you want to alienate. A year later I moved to another organization, and, to my great chagrin, the same woman worked there! She had a different name, different face, etc., but she was a dead ringer for the previous woman I did not like. With some self-examination, I learned what was throwing me about this type of individual. I attempted to change my approach to get along better with a particular type of personality in a co-worker who normally irritated me. It made a huge difference, and she became an ally when I needed to gain access to the CEO. Fortunately, I discovered this nitrogen bubble before it became a major problem.

Neither self-examination nor self-awareness is an end in itself. Both must lead to self-regulation to be truly meaningful. As illustrated in Figure 3.1, Chapter 3, all three of these elements work in concert to make us more effective.

GO DEEPER

Evaluate yourself on six ways to benefit from highly valuable feedback:

1. **Ask for it.** The greater your influence, the less likely others will come to you, especially with critical feedback. Many leaders are "truth starved." We often have to take the initiative and ask for feedback.

   How often do I ask for feedback:

   ☐ Don't remember

   ☐ Seldom

   ☐ Occasionally

   ☐ Often

2. **Listen to it.** Do not interrupt. Do not agree or disagree. Ask questions for greater clarity and insight. If you argue with the feedback provider, it is unlikely you will receive any new feedback of value.

   How well do I listen to feedback:

   ☐ I listen carefully and ask questions for clarification.

   ☐ I listen but don't probe for better understanding.

   ☐ I listen (sort of)—when I don't agree, I tend to ignore the feedback.

   ☐ I am an impatient listener.

☐ I am defensive when I don't agree or don't like the person giving the feedback.

3. **Sit on it.** When you disagree with the feedback, sit on it. Ask some clarifying questions. Be aware of the natural tendency toward self-deception. Process it for a while and remain open to others' perceptions.

When I receive feedback I:

☐ Reflect productively

☐ React immediately

☐ Recoil

4. **Accept it.** Be careful not to come across as defensive when explaining your actions. You might even say, "Let me tell you why I did this. Maybe you can help me find the flaw in my logic."

How well do I accept the feedback:

☐ Embrace it thoughtfully

☐ Deflect it

☐ Inwardly suspect the feedback provider of bias

☐ Wonder if the feedback provider is totally obtuse

5. **Appreciate it.** Express appreciation for what you have been told even when it hurts or when feedback is inconsistent with your self-perception. There is tremendous value in seeing how we exist in the perceptions of others. Thoughtful, wise feedback is a gift. Thank anyone who offers it.

How do I receive feedback:

☐ Appreciatively

☐ Hear it and forget about it

☐ Not so well

6. **Act on it.** Take steps to deal with what you hear and follow up to demonstrate your seriousness about addressing the issue. A sure way to seal off any future feedback is to recriminate those who gave you the feedback.

I act on feedback:

☐ Immediately with conviction

☐ Cautiously with ambivalence

☐ Not likely to do much with the feedback

Based upon your self-evaluation, what are your greatest opportunities to improve your openness to feedback? How will you bring about these changes?

Self-awareness protects our core and makes any leader more prepared to create an impact. The focus of the next chapter is in a specific realm of self-awareness that requires some courage to consider.

CHAPTER 5

SUSTAIN GREAT
LEADERSHIP

"Sustaining an audience is hard. It demands a consistency of thought, of purpose, and of action over a long period of time."

—BRUCE SPRINGSTEEN

O ver the years my work has required travel to a number of countries. I learned early on that exercise helps me get over jet lag, so if the conditions permit, I go running once I get settled into a hotel. Once, a client asked me to attend a meeting at a magnificent resort in a rural jungle area near the South China Sea. After arriving and donning my running clothes, I spoke with the concierge about the best place to jog near the hotel. She smiled and explained that there were only two options.

"Option one is the high road. This is the way you came in from the airport, and as you recall, it is very steep and hilly. There is practically no shade anywhere along the route." The humidity from the nearby jungle was already causing me to sweat profusely, so the thought of running the hills in the hot tropical sun immediately held no appeal.

"Option two," she continued, "is the low road. It is flat, shady, and much cooler because the trade winds blow in from the ocean." Easy decision. As

I turned to leave, she added, ". . . but on the low road you have to be very careful about the monkeys." I watched a lot of Tarzan movies growing up and was not bothered in the slightest by a few "Cheetas" running around. But she was not finished. "These are a particularly aggressive species of monkey, who have bitten and injured a number of people. Yesterday, a golfer had to be rushed to the hospital in Kuala Lumpur."

My only thought now was, "I really need some hill work to get ready for that hot and humid 10K race I plan to run back in the states on July 4th."

TRAVERSING THE LOW ROAD

Most leaders undoubtedly aspire to take the high road. I certainly believe you and I want that. The hardships of the high road can be daunting, but most of the time we push through the barriers and try to do the right thing. Although I want to dwell on the positive aspirations that we share, it is important to understand how a significant number of leaders end up on the low road. Their path is instructive. As my grandmother liked to say, "Nobody's useless. They can at least be used as a bad example."

A crisis of tragic proportions dominates our twenty-four-hour news cycle as prominent leaders in business, government, education, healthcare, ministry, entertainment, sports, and many other fields get plastered across the headlines. Why are so many leaders taking the low road of compromised integrity, when the dangers and certain harm appear obvious to us bystanders? Why do many who reach the pinnacle of their professions risk those metaphorical monkeys who pour out of the jungle to maim their reputations as trustworthy leaders whenever they take the low road? Kenneth Lay, Dennis Kozlowski, Martha Stewart, Anthony Weiner, and General David Petraeus are just a few who were bitten by their own greed or arrogance or narcissism. We ask, "How could he or she have done that? Didn't he realize he would get caught? Why would he risk his reputation and all he has going for him? What was she thinking?"

The scale, frequency, and sheer numbers who have chosen the low road seems far greater today than ever before. A new headline arrives on our doorstep or our iPad almost every day—an increasingly familiar and sordid tale about some leader gone awry.

We wonder about stellar individuals such as Coach Joe Paterno, the 84-year-old former head football coach of Penn State who established more records than anyone in the history of collegiate football, including the most games won and the most national championships.[1] Although he reported an incident to his superior, he was fired in the middle of his final season because he failed to express sufficient moral outrage over a child sex abuse scandal involving one of his assistant coaches. Many believe that Paterno was actively involved in covering up his assistant coach's actions.[2]

WE DO NOT TRUST OUR LEADERS

In America confidence in leaders across the spectrum of business, politics, and religion continues to decline. Harvard's Kennedy School publishes the National Leadership Index.[3] Only the military and the medical community earned above-average confidence scores. Leaders in business, education, religion, government, the news media, and Wall Street all dwell together in the clammy cellar of below-average confidence.

The 2011 Index reveals that 77 percent of Americans believe that we have "a leadership crisis in the country." More than three-quarters of those surveyed also believe that "unless we get better leaders, the United States will decline as a nation." The study's authors conclude with a sobering observation: "Americans' unhappiness with their leaders is approaching the point where it threatens the country's stability and coherence." The 2012 Index showed slight improvement in the overall confidence in our leaders, although those who believe we have a leadership crisis remains quite high at 69 percent. Quite significantly, researchers pointed out that "81 percent of Americans believe the nation's problems can be solved with effective leadership."[4]

Fundamentally, we want to trust our leaders, but when our trust is betrayed, our confidence plummets. We wonder if a few more scandals involving national leaders will somehow push us to a tipping point—will any leader, no matter how effective, have the trust of followers? These failures undermine our trust and make us cynical—why follow anyone?

Could Paterno's downfall have been a failure of courage? Was he reluctant to tip over the Penn State football empire by reporting this outrage regardless of the consequences? Paterno died a few months after the story broke, so we will likely never know Paterno's true motives. We do know that a great American legacy lies in shambles. Paterno's example makes clear that sometimes taking the low road is simply about not speaking up. As Edmund Burke said, "All that is necessary for the triumph of evil is that good men do nothing."

Leadership Is Critically Important

Individuals who exert the disproportionate influence that automatically accompanies a leadership position play such a vital role in virtually every sector of life. The role of leadership is so critical that we must understand the essential elements of great leaders who stay the course.

Strong evidence suggests that it is incredibly difficult to sustain effective leadership over a long period, even after monumental successes.[5] So many individuals of great influence rise only to fall unceremoniously from their lofty perch because of a failure of some dimension of their core, a concept we will look at in depth in the next chapter. A compromised leader diminishes his or her company's potential, and when a leader fails, it places a company or any enterprise at risk. A failed corporate leader demoralizes his or her followers and robs shareholders of immense value.

Our Shadow

We must learn why seemingly good people take the low road of compromised aspirations. More important, we must learn to be aware of our own vulnerabilities for taking the low road. It is not our altruistic motives that get us off track. It is unknown darker motives that create personal havoc.

To foster our impact as a leader, I would be remiss to not acknowledge the reality that, as human beings, we have competing predispositions inside us. Any observer of human nature sees that we have a noble side that clearly seeks to serve the best interest of others. We also have a side that is self-serving. The side of us that we want to disown is called the "shadow," about which the Austrian psychoanalyst Carl Jung wrote extensively. When taken to extreme, this side possesses a dark influence that causes even a normally kind person to be cruel and uncaring. Most leaders with whom I have worked clearly manifest their more positive, noble side. On occasion, I have worked with leaders whose shadow side prevailed. The wreckage and suffering that these leaders cause are memorable and often tragic for those who work in their oppressive organizations. These leaders usually do not endure, but their legacy is often difficult to excise from the organization's culture.

Our culture's obsession with striving to look perfect makes us reluctant to look at our own duality—that some of our impulses are noble, while others are not so benevolent. It is not that we have yielded to our shadow, but we prefer to deny that we even *have* a shadow.

Maybe we acknowledge our shadow in a detached, abstract way, but to really open the door and look at our shadow side is not so easy. We might admit to having a small shadow. Even in our most glaringly candid moments we are reluctant to acknowledge that some of our inclinations are, at least, ineffective, if not dishonorable. Denial provides a safe way to sidestep our tension—or at least it seems that way. One of those craggy ancient prophets put it more tersely: "The human heart is the most deceitful of all things . . ."[6] We are better served to not deceive ourselves, because acknowledging our shadow lessens its unconscious power over us.

Even in our most glaringly candid moments
we are reluctant to acknowledge that some of
our inclinations are, at least, ineffective, if not
dishonorable. Denial provides a safe way to sidestep
our tension—or at least it seems that way.

If you are having trouble believing you have a shadow, download the very funny movie *Liar Liar*.[7] Jim Carrey's character, Fletcher Reede, is an attorney who lies all the time. He lies to his clients, his friends, and even his young son. He never keeps his commitments. His son makes a birthday wish that his father would stop lying for a day. The wish comes true, and Fletcher finds himself uncontrollably telling the truth every moment. The contortions Carrey goes through to censor what's really inside of him are hilarious, but they also make us a bit uncomfortable. What would it would be like if we always expressed what is inside of us completely unvarnished?

In moments of gut-wrenching candor, many self-aware leaders acknowledge their shadow. Leaders who have great strengths also possess significant weaknesses, which cannot be ignored. Sadly, we, too, have the innate capacity for narcissism, arrogance, or disregard of other's opinions and interests in favor of our own. Perceptive executives control these impulses and choose to manage their shadow's intrusion on decisions and relationships. Others—through blindness or foolish disregard—do not. Those who are more likely to stay out of trouble constantly remind themselves of their own vulnerability.

Shakespeare's *Macbeth* reveals that the aspirations of our shadow side can compromise even the purest of souls. "Vaulting ambition, which o'er leaps itself/And falls on th' other [side]."[8]

When we live the grayness of conflicted motives (as most of us do), we miss the clarity of the noonday sun and lose perspective about what's right, but if and when we're willing to put some light on our own less-admirable qualities, it becomes painfully apparent that we all have the latent potential to take the low road.

---

*Those who are more likely to stay out of
trouble constantly remind themselves
of their own vulnerability.*

Finding the High Road

I am convinced that most leaders want to stay on the high road. They began their careers with idealistic aspirations for making an impact, but, over time, power and the trappings of success erode those convictions. Choosing to take the low road is rarely a precipitous move. Rather, it is a gradual progression over time.

In an earlier book, *Derailed*, I documented that whenever someone falls from greatness, there are five predictable stages, which are as follows:

1. Lack of self-awareness
2. Arrogance or misguided confidence
3. Missed warning signals
4. Rationalization
5. Derailment[9]

In an upcoming chapter, I will draw particular attention to the fourth stage, rationalization, which sends us barreling down the low road in a hurry. Rationalization is a dark emotional incubator that nurtures "rational lies." We lie convincingly to ourselves about our behavior and also ignore or minimize feedback from others. The arrogance and inherently self-serving message of these lies blind us to the clear warning signals of our impending doom.

By the time stage five hits, we reach the end of the line. The consequences vary widely, but it is certainly unlikely we will remain in our present role.

Well-adjusted people have this inner tension between dueling natures, but we will not dwell on our shadow. One aim of this book is to avoid, at any cost, going down the path of personal destruction like a few of the leaders mentioned earlier in this chapter. The great news is that simply acknowledging our shadow helps us to minimize its impact. We can then better focus on strengthening our core.

In the next chapter, we will learn the force that makes us most vulnerable to our darker instincts and how to mitigate its influence.

CHAPTER 6

DANGER—
HIGH VOLTAGE

"Great men are almost always bad."

—LORD ACTON

Those old grainy black-and-white films still haunt me—the ones of Hiroshima, after the crew of a B-29 bomber called the *Enola Gay* dropped an atomic bomb on the city toward the end of World War II: the mushroom cloud followed by the firestorm and the absolute devastation to the city and its inhabitants. All we see is rubble, a few tree stumps, and dead bodies for miles in every direction. That event galvanized the world's attention. People everywhere suddenly became aware of the exponential power of nuclear energy, and they feared what could happen if it were misdirected or carelessly controlled.

Today we worry about Iran developing the bomb. We are apprehensive about what a terrorist could do with a suitcase-sized nuclear device. We are incredulous when really smart people design a fail-safe system, like the one at the Fukushima nuclear power plant, that turns out to be so vulnerable. By placing the power generators for the backup cooling pumps on the beach below the reactor building, they practically dared the 2011 tsunami that struck Japan to slam into this nuclear plant.

Nuclear power plants are designed to meet the standards of multiple stress tests—various scenarios that have the potential, individually or in combination, to overload a plant's safety systems. If the operating protocols and containment structures of a nuclear power plant are compromised either by human error or the forces of nature, the results can be catastrophic. The Tōhoku earthquake in 2011 (9.0 on the Richter scale) and its resulting 133-foot tsunami did just that.[1]

Still, the enormous benefits of nuclear power compel many countries to continue its use. A relatively small nuclear plant can power millions of homes and businesses with minimal carbon emissions. In fact, France derives 80 percent of its electricity from nuclear energy.[2] And in the United States the safety record of nuclear plants is excellent.[3]

Nuclear power remains such a controversial topic because although it poses considerable risks and dangers, like the threat of a terrorist attack or the recent meltdown in Japan, it also provides a substantial amount of clean energy.

PERSONAL POWER AND THE STRESS TEST

Like nuclear power, the power we exercise over others holds enormous potential to be either productive or destructive. Initially, as we gain power, our aspirations are positive and we expect to use it to do great things. Unfortunately, many with power today are simply not passing the stress test.

The purpose of this chapter is to alert us to how power can unintentionally mold us into someone we do not want to be and to highlight the containment structures and safety protocols we need to use power well. First, we need to consider how a leader actually gets power. In human endeavors, power emanates from a variety of sources.

SOURCES OF POWER

The position and title a person holds in an organization bestows power. This is true for all positions. Even the guy in the mailroom has some power because of his position, which allows him to dispense or withhold something we want. The one with the most positional power in an organization, other than the board of directors, is the chief executive officer.

Power also flows from having knowledge, skill, and expertise. I know a consultant to the paper industry who visited a plant for five minutes and charged the company $15,000. He justified his high fee because he was the only one who knew that the scrubbers on their malfunctioning smokestacks were upside down. Technical experts like information technology workers who solve big problems and control huge resources have significant power based upon what they know.

We can also be powerful because of who we know or represent. This type of power results from being connected in some way to powerful people. We have likely experienced this power, because we sometimes gain access to people or resources that our own standing would not permit. Our connection to powerful people and use of another person's name can open doors that we cannot.

Influence is also a type of power. A leader with influence holds sway over others not from position but rather from persuasion. Whether for good or bad, effective or ineffective, we exercise power over those we influence. Power often attends anyone with ideas and vision that capture the imagination of others. Consider Martin Luther King, Jr., who exercised power over millions of people because he had a dream that resonated with the hopes and aspirations of so many. Bernie Madoff also had great influence, but he used his power for very dark, self-serving ends.

A leader with influence holds sway over others not from position but rather from persuasion.

Many corporate executives understand the power of influence because it increasingly has played a major role in how corporations function. As organizational structures become flatter and more matrixed, managers accomplish the work of their organization by influencing co-workers over whom they have no formal authority. Learning to use this type of power well is a critical skill in many organizations.

Power derived from influence on the surface may seem nobler and less subject to its corrupting effect. In fact, with the power of influence we are no less vulnerable than if we have a position of power.

POWER CORRUPTS

Most people who derive power from any of the above sources are not bad—they are often good people with good intentions. Individuals on the rise in organizations often exhibit discipline, good judgment, respect for others, and similar redeeming qualities. Managers with these qualities tend to be promoted in organizations. These positive characteristics along with the achievement of results help them advance into higher levels of leadership. Surprisingly, many of these once agreeable individuals who find themselves in positions of significant power display a radical shift in their behavior. They become dismissive of others, aloof, self-important, and, at times, even reckless. After they occupy a higher level job for a while, the unanticipated pressures of the position can overwhelm their personal containment systems, marring their promising careers.

Regardless of the source, power can be directed to benefit others or to pursue a more self-serving purpose. Its very nature puts our core motivations at risk. Power contains certain spores, which if inhaled can mold us and lead to an unruly self-focus. Lord Acton's well-known quote states it more bluntly: "Power . . . corrupt[s] . . ."

As I write this, a huge scandal is emerging. Early reports indicate the U.S. Internal Revenue Service abused its authority by targeting certain groups for audits or added processing steps purely for political purposes.[4] Although much remains to be learned about what actually happened and who was responsible, it seems clear that power breached the core of some leaders. Unregulated power of any type has that effect. Arrogance and a self-serving focus are the frequent consequences.

Although power is inherently neither good nor bad, unregulated power is a highly potent force that can exert an insidious effect on our core when we obtain it. For most people, power is acquired slowly, and therefore, its core-altering effect is subtle. Power is odorless and tasteless like carbon monoxide and can overpower us without warning. This force maintains a growing pressure on our volition, and absent thoughtful reflection and purposeful containment, we unthinkingly begin using this force to advance self-serving ends.

We will likely never know exactly why fired CIA head and former four-star general David Petraeus went off the rails, but we would have to put power high on the list of suspects. Four-star generals are not well paid by corporate standards, but the perks are amazing: armored limousine, personal driver, jets, and a huge staff. Navigating the thirty years or so it takes to reach that rank is incredibly demanding and dangerous. As officers rise in rank, they become increasingly insular, surrounded mostly by a staff who needs their position to get promoted—not exactly an incubator for contrary ideas. It is very easy for the power to erode their core. The self-focus that power fosters can lead to a perceived sense of self-importance. After all their achievements, perhaps it becomes easy for senior officers to believe that they are great and have risen above the rules.[5]

Influential people we admire and view as trustworthy are not immune to power's potential impact to their core—nor are we. Once tasted, our appetite for power can grow. Power can be highly addictive. A newly minted CEO told me that he experienced a creeping dark sway of his newly bestowed power oozing into his actions. He did not like who he was becoming—that he was beginning to see others as a means to an end, and that he was constantly expecting others to serve him. Fortunately, his self-awareness served as an early-warning system, so that he could make some dramatic changes to contain the influence of the power he assumed with his new position and title.

---

*Once tasted, our appetite for power can
grow. Power can be highly addictive.*

POWER CAN BE SELF-RIGHTEOUS

In one study, psychologists asked members of a high-power group about speeding. The group concluded that it was okay for them to speed, but that it was important for others to follow the posted limit. Their rationale was that powerful people are important and had a justifiable reason for speeding.[6] It seems the more powerful we become, the more likely we are to overestimate our own moral virtue, and then paradoxically, to act in a morally expedient manner.

Unchecked power fuels arrogance and the belief that we are smarter and more capable than, in reality, we may be. Under no circumstance should we ever act like the leader in the cartoon on the following page.

As we become more powerful, we rely too much on our intuition, possibly ignoring the facts and the input of others that served us so effectively during our ascent. We tend to overreach and make bad decisions.

Regardless of our position on America's involvement in Mid-East wars, most would affirm that many noble, heroic, and selfless acts have been performed in the attempt to liberate Iraq and Afghanistan. By contrast, we were shocked and dismayed to see U.S. military guards acting shamefully at Abu Ghraib prison in Iraq. We wonder how presumably good, moral, well-intentioned soldiers could treat military prisoners with utter disregard for their basic human dignity. Although the explanations are complex and differ from one person to another, suffice it to say that power possesses great potential for good or evil. Unregulated power can erode our ethical underpinnings. Any compromise to our core makes us vulnerable to dark motives, and power provides a potent fuel for those motives.

"Some people, Remson, are born to push the envelope, and some are born to lick it."

WHAT IF WE WERE PRISON GUARDS?

One famous study, the Stanford Prison Experiment, demonstrated how power molds our attitudes toward others. The bottom floor of Stanford University's psychology building became a temporary "prison," and student volunteers were designated as either "prisoners" or "guards." After being arrested, the prisoners were held in small cells. The psychology professor who led the study, Philip Zimbardo, was shocked at how quickly the experimental subjects adopted their roles. Most notably, within the first two days many of those imbued with the power of being guards became abusive, hostile, and dehumanizing toward the prisoners. The behavioral changes in the guards and the prisoners were so stunning that the planned two-week experiment had to be suspended after six days, particularly to avert the prisoners' extreme stress reactions.[7] If nothing else, this study confirms how easily and quickly unregulated power can corrupt us.

Sometimes I wonder if airport screening has become a gargantuan Stanford Prison Experiment. Although I deeply appreciate the stress-filled role that well-meaning TSA agents play in keeping us safe when we fly, I cannot help but notice how the power inherent in the position seems to affect the judgment and attitude of some agents. I am revolted when an agent violates basic decency and common sense by insisting a 95-year-old grandmother remove her incontinence diaper for inspection.[8] I often encounter friendly, service-minded agents, but many others seem to believe arrogance and rudeness are job requirements. Unchecked power can have that effect on anyone.

Responsible Use of Power

Members of an organization typically grow in power over the course of their careers. Self-awareness and self-regulation must grow in direct proportion to the power we exert.

The responsible use of power must be intentionally cultivated over time and through experience. Many companies go to great lengths to groom and train younger associates to develop the critical competencies they need to perform at the next level or two in the organization. Job experience and feedback from insightful bosses often prepare a person to handle power more responsibly. Giving an emerging leader power in small increments also helps develop responsible leaders. When the development process works well, it teaches a young associate that the purpose of power is to implement strategies and to reach difficult goals while valuing and respecting the team that accomplishes the goals.

The purpose of power is to implement strategies and to reach difficult goals while valuing and respecting the team that accomplishes the goals.

Recently I have been studying the progress of a young executive with interest. He has a major responsibility in a growing company, but no one reports to him. He can only get things done through influence. I believe the CEO is wise to give this talented individual a lot of responsibility while also making it essential that he cultivate good relationships with the colleagues whose support he must have to accomplish his objectives. It's only a matter of time before this promising young individual does have a position of power over others, but he will have learned the benefits of creating alignment with others to get things done. This is an effective development process to help him learn to handle power responsibly.

Feedback from an insightful boss can also prove vital in helping us learn to use power with care. A good friend who was gung ho about his job and determined to prove his merit would often call people at home to discuss work-related matters. When his boss found out, he gave him some very tough feedback about respecting his employees' personal boundaries. He said that, unless the building was on fire, to never interrupt someone's dinner hour again. After serving in numerous roles, my friend eventually went on to be the CEO of a major company. By then, he had learned to handle power responsibly and demonstrated great self-awareness about the potential abuses of it.

Over the years I have worked with a number of family-owned businesses. A common problem I see is when a family member (often the child or grandchild of the owner) gets placed in a role and receives a title that exceeds his or her experience and competence. The family member who is given a role and assumes power not commensurate with his or her maturity typically does not have a strongly developed core—one forged in the furnace of experience to regulate their power well. When an organization bestows a position or title on an emerging leader who everyone knows is not equipped to handle the power inherent in the role responsibly, employees do not respect or trust that leader. That person is also much more vulnerable to power's dark influence.

Recent findings from brain research also support the idea that emerging leaders should be given power in a more measured way based upon maturity. Areas of the brain responsible for planning, prioritizing, and controlling impulses are the last to mature.[9] We can probably recall our own personal illustrations demonstrating this phenomenon! If memory fails you, call your parents or siblings or your high school friends for some good examples.

When we are not prepared to handle power well, the consequences are often harsh. One afternoon during a family vacation, I walked in from the surf with my back to the ocean oblivious to a fifteen-foot rogue wave towering over me. Suddenly, I was slammed to the ocean floor so hard that the breath was knocked out of me. Then I was run through what felt like the spin cycle of an industrial-strength washing machine and sandblasted over every square inch of my body. Gaining power in whatever role we serve puts us at a great risk when the power commensurate with our role is not used carefully. If we turn our back to those inherent dangers, we can be knocked to the floor by an unanticipated tsunami of events from which we may never recover.

THE ULTIMATE TEST

Abraham Lincoln said, "Nearly all men can stand adversity, but if you want to test a man's character, give him power." Power is dangerous and should be handled with great care. If the containment structure of our core is undeveloped, we have to be especially vigilant. An undeveloped core is like the levees around New Orleans during Hurricane Katrina. They could not contain the storm's power. We live in a volatile, unpredictable world in which many of the conventional rules of corporate governance have failed to contain and direct many leaders' power. Today, as perhaps never before, corporate leaders must possess an extraordinarily resilient core to pass the stress tests that the marketplace metes out so freely.

"Nearly all men can stand adversity,
but if you want to test a man's
character, give him power."

—ABRAHAM LINCOLN

Examples of stress tests that we must be ready to handle are:

- How we handle disagreements with those who report to us.
- How we handle disagreements with peers in our organization.
- Our willingness to be accountable to others for our decisions and actions.
- The temptation to take personal credit for results others have achieved.
- Ensuring that our actions serve the best interests of the organization versus promoting our own advancement.

We may not feel that we are vulnerable to power's dark effect because it is often too subtle to detect. This obscures the reality that within all of us the seeds for susceptibility are sewn. As we established in Chapter 5, we have a shadow. When we exercise the courage to admit to ourselves that all our motives are not necessarily altruistic and noble, we have taken a crucial step in the profound journey toward the impact we earnestly seek to achieve.

I spoke with a senior officer of a company recently. He openly confessed that he worries that he could get caught up in his own importance and miss the right ways to lead his company and serve its members. He acknowledged that he could easily wake up one morning and find that he had blindly followed a path to his own personal destruction. When we possess power, self-examination and self-awareness serve like safety protocols in a nuclear plant, prompting us to consider the condition of our personal core.

SAFE HARNESSING

The safe harnessing of power is fundamental to being a great leader who makes an impact. We must intentionally examine ourselves. We need to look deep to ask if we are controlling power or if power is controlling us. We must appreciate that our assumption of power has immense potential to help us make a positive difference in the lives of those we serve or to drive us to narcissistic self-interest. We must adopt "operating protocols" and "safety systems" to assuage power's erosion of our core. We must wrap this force in a containment structure channeling whatever power we might have in directions that serve the common good. Safety systems and containment structures to protect our personal core are the topics for the remainder of the book. If such protections are not put in place, we too will inevitably become one of Lord Acton's powerful but bad people.

When we use power for self-serving ends we often get compliance from those we lead, but we do not engage their commitment to willingly follow us. Reflect on how you use power and in what ways you need to make some changes. Power is best used to serve others. Its careful regulation is the subject of the next chapter.

GO DEEPER

I use power to _____.
(check all boxes which apply):

☐ Get my way when I know I'm right.

☐ Move things along when there's not time for debate.

☐ Periodically remind others who's in charge.

☐ Get things done when I'm too fatigued or stressed-out to listen to input.

☐ Help my team get through some external roadblocks to solve a problem for a customer.

☐ As a position from which to serve the members of my organization to help them get their jobs done.

CHAPTER 7

Make Sure Those Wires Have Good Insulation

"First pride, then the crash—
the bigger the ego, the harder the fall."[1]

—ANCIENT PROVERB

I will never forget the news conference in which Democratic Senate candidate Martha Coakley fielded questions from reporters. At the time, Scott Brown, her opponent in the special election following Massachusetts Senator Ted Kennedy's death in 2009, was rapidly gaining ground in the polls. The outcome was important nationally because if Coakley lost, Senate Democrats forfeited their ability to shut off a filibuster. Coakley, however, was overconfident because many considered her victory to be guaranteed. When a reporter asked if she planned to step up her somewhat passive campaign efforts, Coakley shot back, "What do you expect me to do, go over to Fenway Park and shake hands with people in the cold?"[2]

Whether you supported Coakley's candidacy or not, you would probably want to say, "Well, yes, Martha, you probably should go meet the people you intend to represent!" Her statement in both tone and sentiment dripped with narcissism and arrogance. How could she fail to see that

73

her statement (and more important the belief behind it) would seal her doom? Did she not even care about how contemptuously her comments would be viewed?

Scott Brown meanwhile drove all over Massachusetts for many months in an old pickup truck meeting the voters, and he soundly defeated Coakley for the coveted U.S. Senate seat. Coakley had done what many considered impossible—lose the Kennedy seat to an upstart. Voters really did not like Coakley's arrogance and proved it when they temporarily put Brown in the job. It was clear to even her most ardent supporters that Coakley had moved beyond typical arrogance to its more extreme form—hubris.

THE HIGH COST OF ARROGANCE

In the ancient Greek culture, hubris denoted insolence and even violence. Acting in a superior manner and belittling others was a crime in Greek culture. Greek plays portrayed characters with hubris as having a fatal flaw—they always met their demise.[3] Coakley seemed like a modern-day version of a flawed character from a Greek tragedy. Her arrogance blinded her to her vulnerabilities. Her lack of respect for the voters in Massachusetts caused her to lose the Kennedy seat to a Republican.

The Greeks coined the word *hubris*, but other cultures also condemned the terrible flaw of arrogance. Obadiah, a Hebrew prophet, told an overconfident nation of Israel, "You have been deceived by your own pride."[4]

There is a clear connection between overconfidence and moral failure. Arrogance often results from unbridled power. Power pushes us toward an unruly self-focus and fosters beliefs that are simply not true. Lord Acton's observation that "Power corrupts" recognizes that there is something about the nature of unregulated power that gets inside us and subtly influences our beliefs. Then we start believing really dumb things like, "I don't have to follow the normal rules."

Wisdom recognizes our vulnerability and prompts a vigilant inventory of anything that leads to arrogance, abuse of power, faulty assumptions about our own importance, or decisions guided by self-serving impulses. As noble as our intentions might be as we assume a leadership role, we are always one errant, unthinking action or careless word away from getting outside the boundaries of good judgment or even the moral absolutes that must frame all decisions.

As noble as our intentions might be as we assume a leadership role, we are always one errant, unthinking action or careless word away from getting outside the boundaries of good judgment or even the moral absolutes that must frame all decisions.

As we discussed in Chapter 5, outright failure and the short tenures of many leaders have become all too common. A position of leadership is more fragile than we might believe. General Petraeus, for example, served as director of the CIA for only thirteen months before he was brought down by a lapse in judgment.

Arrogance is a corrosive element that erodes our core. It results from unmonitored and unchecked power. You may remember a high school chemistry lab experiment that shows how a metal plate is turned to mush by sulfuric acid. Arrogance is the ultimate sulfuric acid poured upon the steel plate guarding our core.

How specifically does arrogance harm our core? First, arrogance is a major obstacle to self-awareness. It cuts off the information so critical to the regulation of power. Coakley simply could not see the hubris in her "take it for granted" campaign efforts. She possessed a huge blind spot with respect to how her behavior affronted voters in her state.

Second, arrogance also deceives us. Coakley had served for many years as Massachusetts Attorney General and thought she deserved the Senate seat—she was entitled. She apparently did not see that she had to continue to earn voters' trust.

Third, arrogance distances us from others. We can become aloof to the interests and needs of others. It causes us to believe that as a leader, we are placed in a position to be served by others versus being in a role from which we serve. Followers do not trust leaders who will not mingle with the rest of us. Bob Nardelli, former CEO of Home Depot, commandeered an elevator in the lobby of the home office building such that it went from his personal parking place in the basement straight to his office on the top floor without stopping at any other floors. Employees naturally resented this, and the elevator became a glaring symbol of his arrogance. The board eventually fired Nardelli because, among other factors, employees did not engage with his vision. His arrogance obscured their ability to see where he wanted to take the company.

Arrogance distances the very people we need to help us accomplish our vision. Video conferencing is a wonderful technology, but it is also easy for a leader to develop the "Wizard of Oz syndrome"—a leader behind a curtain somewhere. Do not be like Nardelli, who stayed on the top floor of the Home Depot office building and ate only in the executive dining room with the private chef. Be present with the people you want to lead as often as possible. Be visible. Eat in the regular cafeteria with normal folks whenever your schedule permits.

We also have to be really conscious of verbal references. I consulted with a company for a number of years in which the leader frequently in private and public referred to his very large department as "Ladies on floor." At the time, the overwhelming majority of his employees were women who handled largely clerical tasks. The managers were mainly men. I know it is only three words strung together, but the thoughtless arrogance that phrase implied was stunning. In many cases, organizations develop shorthand references for communicating expediently; however, be careful what a shorthand reference such as "Ladies on floor" might inadvertently convey.

We must be intentional about how we want others to feel in our organization. I often recommend executives not have reserved parking places. Sure, the convenience is nice, but those signs that say "Reserved for the President" invite perceptions that she is "a cut above the rest of us." Do we want followers to feel that we are more intelligent than they are? Do we want them to be sure they treat us like the big kahuna? If yes, we are certain to find a way. If we *instead* want people to feel affirmed and valued, then we must look at them, listen to them, and thank them and treat them as equals.

Our nonverbal communication is critical. Recently I observed a bank executive who actually purported to value humility. As he spoke, his head went back and each finger and thumb on one hand touched the corresponding finger and thumb on his other hand. He held this pyramid of fingers just under his chin and looked very professorial. Others visibly recoiled at the arrogance captured in the nonverbal signals he sent. Our body language seldom lies and may unconsciously reveal our shadow. As noted earlier in the book, lack of self-awareness can get us in trouble in a hurry.

THAT VERY DANGEROUS GAME OF WHO GETS CREDIT

As we grow in power and influence, arrogance has the potential to promote an undeserved overconfidence that falsely convinces us, "*I* did this." We overestimate the importance of our own contribution and ignore or diminish the contributions of others. Humility is an honest acknowledgment of the truth about me, my capabilities, and my role, while simultaneously recognizing the contributions of others. Mike Volkema, chairman of Herman Miller, the manufacturer of high-end office furniture, told me that, in his experience, members of a team who promote their own interests too aggressively or take individual credit for what a team accomplished "get cut from the herd pretty quickly."[5]

A guy who worked in my firm years ago used to dominate meetings with his comments on everything. Lack of knowledge or expertise never proved to be a barrier to his weighing in on a topic. Most of his contributions felt more like a lecture. Other team members complained to me about his arrogance. I sat down with him one day to point out his rapidly diminishing credibility with the team. He explained that in his previous firm, the person who commanded the most air time in meetings won the best assignments and garnered the most respect from the team. He had not embraced the very different culture in our firm, where shameless self-promotion worked against his interests. Unfortunately my feedback did not work, and he was soon cut from the herd.

THE ANECDOTE TO ARROGANCE

It has been well-documented that humility is a characteristic of great leaders, but an important question is why. Essentially, humility is a key preventative that keeps us from going down that terrible path of personal destruction we see too often in leaders. If arrogance is the mother of all derailers, then humility is the mother of all safeguards.

If arrogance is the mother of all derailers, then humility is the mother of all safeguards.

We sometimes get confused about humility, thinking that we have to diminish ourselves to be humble. C. S. Lewis said, "Humility isn't thinking less of yourself, it's thinking of yourself less." Humility acknowledges that arrogance brings us down in a hurry. We should feel good about a significant accomplishment, but it should not foster that arrogant form of pride that says, "I'm the smartest guy in the room and deserve credit for this accomplishment." Guarding our core means we must keep arrogance at bay. Confidence is desirable, but we need to avoid slipping into over-confidence. It may be hard to define technically where the line is, but we generally know it when we see it. Great leaders affirm others frequently for their contributions to a given outcome.

"Humility isn't thinking less of yourself,
it's thinking of yourself less."

—C. S. LEWIS

I don't know about you, but humility has, at times, seemed a bit squishy to me. I grew up watching Clint Eastwood movies. Harry Callahan is the iconic tough guy, and, trust me, "Dirty" Harry is not humble. When he chases down the bad guys, he is dangerous:

> I know what you're thinking, punk. You're thinking, "Did he fire six shots or only five?" Now to tell you the truth, I forgot myself in all this excitement. But being this is a forty-four Magnum, the most powerful handgun in the world and will blow your head clean off, you've gotta ask yourself one question: "Do I feel lucky?" Well, do ya, punk?[6]

Yeah, Harry, pull that trigger. We love a maverick, because they live on the edge and keep us unsettled. The only problem is that this is not how normal people really live. People usually do not follow a maverick. They just observe him or her with great interest, wondering how long it will be before the maverick implodes. People follow a leader they trust, not one who provides great entertainment value.

Naval officers often refer to the "integrity of the hull." When a submarine comes out of dry dock, the first exercise is called a "sea trial," which takes the submarine to depth in the ocean to test the integrity of the hull. If integrity is compromised in any way, such as a poor weld, the stress from the increased pressure of deep water will inevitably find that weakness.

Some of the toughest, most resilient leaders I know are also incredibly humble. Humility is not weakness. Rather, humility is personal armor that wraps around our core like the hull of a submarine. Inside a submarine are people, sophisticated electronics, weapons, and the nuclear reactor core, all of which need protection. Likewise, humility must be strong and all-encompassing to protect our personal core from the inevitable stressors in our lives.

POWER USED WELL

Perhaps most important, humility protects us from the pernicious influence of power. Humility places a governor on our power, so that we use it in measured quantities. Recently a gifted young manager who had worked his way up the organization chart over a number of years in a client company was promoted. He now reported directly to the CEO and had a huge responsibility. The break room talk even whispered his name as a candidate for the CEO's position at some point in the future. I watched with interest over a number of months to see how he would handle his newfound power and how his new peers would accept him. He handled the transition masterfully because he was humble—a characteristic he had exemplified since entering the company some years before. He was self-deprecating in a humorous way and reached out for help from his peers to learn his new responsibilities. He also continued to relate well to the managers at his previous level. It actually made people like him more and affirmed the CEO's judgment in promoting him to the larger role in the company. Be vigilant to not let power provoke its insidious distortion of your importance.

One of the greatest stories in ancient literature tells of a woman who had great impact, because her power was enveloped in humility. Full of deception and intrigue, this story also reminds us of a reality TV show. A young woman named Esther becomes queen to the most powerful monarch of the day. How Esther came about this position sounds like an early version of *The Bachelor*.

The story begins with the previous queen arrogantly embarrassing the king in front of his friends—not a smart move. She is sent packing, and a search begins for a new queen. Scouts gather eligible young women from provinces around the kingdom to compete in a beauty contest with a large number of contestants. The king picks Esther, clearly the hottest of the group, to be the new queen, and all the other contestants get voted off the island (am I mixing up TV shows here?).

The plot thickens, and a diabolical villain who hates a particular race of people conspires to murder all the members of that race living in Persia. The villain, who works for the king, guilefully organizes legislation to legitimize their genocide, not knowing that Esther is a descendant of the race for which he intends ill.

As the narrative unfolds, we learn that besides being beautiful and charming, Esther recognizes that she has been made queen for a purpose—to protect the lives of thousands of people. Esther demonstrates tremendous courage by risking everything to save this group of oppressed people. She realizes that she could ignore the villain's schemes, keep her racial background a secret and just be rich, enjoy her position as queen, and have an easy life. Instead she wants her existence to count for more than ease and recognizes that she exists for a purpose that transcends her own comfort.

Esther seeks to influence the king, even though her uninvited pursuit of the king's audience is a capital crime unless he intervenes. Just before she crosses the threshold that may end her life, Esther's adoptive father challenges her with the idea that she lives "for such a time as this." She resolves, "If I perish, I perish."

A variety of factors contributed to Esther's impact. Certainly her beauty, intelligence, political skill, and courage were vital, but her humility garnered the king's loyalty and respect. She could have stormed into the king's chamber and demanded justice for an oppressed people. Rather, she showed great respect and deference in how she approached him. Humility undergirded her every word and action.

Fortunately for many thousands of people about to be exterminated, Esther's humble petition moved the heart of the king. Justice prevailed, her people were spared, and the villain was hung on the seventy-five-foot gallows he intended for Esther's adoptive father.

You either have or likely will have significant power at some point in your career. A question we must ask ourselves is do we have our power and the arrogance that can accompany it fully in check. Some of the most important tests in our lives usually do not have a long runway. They suddenly appear, and we have our own moment "for such a time as this." The exercises below may help you gauge your readiness.

GO DEEPER

We cringe at the thought of some guy writing a book called "Humility and How I Obtained It," so I will not pretend to be an expert. Here are some humbly offered ideas. Rate yourself on the following:

1. I acknowledge my vulnerability to arrogance particularly when I possess power.

1	2	3	4	5
Not at All Vulnerable		Moderate Vulnerability		Highly Vulnerable

2. I give credit where credit is due.

1	2	3	4	5
I take full credit for projects in my area.		I take full credit for projects in my area but recognize the contribution of others.		I make certain the team and its members get full acknowledgment for what they accomplished.

3. I pay attention to my verbal references (e.g., "Ladies on Floor").

1	2	3	4	5
No attention to verbal references		Some monitoring of my verbal references		Very tuned into verbal references and possible unintended consequences

4. I monitor my body language.

1	2	3	4	5
No attention to my body language		Some monitoring of my body language		Very tuned into my body language

5. I move toward others, not away.

1	2	3	4	5
I keep a professional distance from the people I lead.		I try to be with the people I lead a good bit.		I am a highly visible leader who is very engaged with people in the organization.

6. I have symbols of power.

1	2	3	4	5
Symbols of power are good.... I have lots of them.		I have a few symbols of power.		I work hard to avoid symbols of power.

7. I have others around me who will speak truth to power.

1	2	3	4	5
Everyone around me is a complete lackey.		There are a few people who give me their honest opinion.		My colleagues at work give me their honest opinions and hold me accountable for my actions.

8. I am approachable and welcome feedback from others, including people who are "lower" on the org chart.

1	2	3	4	5
I've made it clear in actions and words that I really don't want to know what others think.		Every now and then I try to get my boss's opinion about how I'm doing.		I have fostered a culture of openness and directness. Anyone can express any opinion to me.

9. I am thoughtful and intentional about how I want people around me to feel.

1	2	3	4	5
I want people around me to know their place.		I show some interest in the members of my team.		I go out of my way to convey to others that they are critical to the success of our organization.

10. I sincerely believe humility is a critical ingredient for successful leaders.

1	2	3	4	5
No thanks.		I see some some value in this.		This is a personal development priority.

Scoring Instructions for the Humility Survey:

1. Add your scores on the ten items.
2. Calibrate how you did on the following ranges:

    46–50   Excellent

    36–45   Good

26–35   Fair

20–25   Needs attention

<20   Needs some immediate attention

3. Create an action plan as to how you become more authentically humble.

☐ Identify two to three actions you will begin to implement this important discipline.

☐ Determine when you will start.

☐ Determine how can you be accountable to someone to make this discipline a habit.

In our charisma-driven culture, being humble may not be cool and hip, but it sure beats the cratering of our careers and lives. A universal principle is implied in the opening quote of this chapter, but particularly for leaders, arrogance is the mother of all derailers. This book is about protecting our core and making the impact for which we hope. Humility performs a critical role in protecting us from the terrible dangers of arrogance, power, and self-absorption. Be vigilant about humility.

CHAPTER 8

WHAT DO YOU *REALLY* BELIEVE?

"For as [a person] thinks within himself, so he is . . ."[1]

—ANCIENT PROVERB

My wife, Anne, has a primordial fear of bugs. I do not know how she developed this fear, but her terror persisted over the years despite my best attempts to cure her. She believed that bugs would do something dreadful to her. No bug has ever, in fact, assaulted her, but her unbridled fear remained. When I was finishing graduate school, we lived in a rented home that had seen some better days. She would enter a dark room, flip on the light, see a bug on the floor, and let out a Hollywood-quality, blood-curdling scream.

Our four-year-old son watched her reaction several times, and one night I saw him have the same response to a bug. His scream was identical down to the note. The quality of reproduction was stunning. Anne and I agreed that her passing this fear to our son was not a great parental legacy, so for his sake, we needed to quickly change his emerging beliefs about bugs as objects of fear. She changed her behavior because she realized that if she did not change, our son was going to become a bug-fearing, neurotic wuss (this was my formal clinical diagnosis). Being a "good mother" is a strong motivator, so she had a reason to change to help her son.

To change his beliefs about bugs, we adopted a biological curiosity approach, like, "Wow, look how many legs he has. What do you suppose she's doing with those antennas?" We tried to catch bugs and put them in glass jars for further study. This technique actually worked, and today our son is a world-famous professor of entomology. Just kidding. He is actually a commercial real estate developer, but he is not afraid of bugs.

Anne saw bugs as a threat—in reality, the bugs were not going to hurt her, but because she *believed* they would she acted in accordance with her belief. When she saw one, she felt afraid, screamed, and ran. Her belief about bugs ("They are going to hurt me") drove her actions (running) and her feelings (fear and revulsion). However, her "I need to be a good mother and role model" belief supplanted her "Bugs are going to hurt me" belief. Our son was starting to react the same way until we fostered different beliefs in him, which, in turn, resulted in very different behavior—curiosity, amusement, etc.

Anne is still not a big fan of bugs, but she has done a lot better at controlling her fear. I thought she might revert to her old self when our sons went off to college, but she handles the occasional bug pretty well. Ralph, her bug guy, also does a good job of keeping them out of our house in the first place.

BE CAREFUL WHAT YOU BELIEVE

The bug example is a simple, personal illustration of how beliefs determine our behavior, both our actions and our emotions. The exact same principles apply to leadership. Our beliefs play a tremendous role in determining how we act as leaders. I often ask leaders what they believe about the people who work in their organization. Although they may use less offensive words, some leaders believe that followers are fundamentally lazy, trying to do no more than necessary to keep their jobs, and as a result require close supervision. "Workers do not do what you expect, but only what you inspect." For these leaders, threat and coercion are primary management tools.

Contrast these leaders with the ones who believe that most followers are self-motivated, generally conscientious, want to do a good job, are fundamentally well-intentioned, and driven to fulfill the mission of the organization. Given the right conditions, followers will be largely self-managed and seek positive outcomes. These leaders say, "If they have the necessary information and training, followers will usually make good decisions and require only broad oversight from management."

I have met many leaders in different industries with one or the other of the two sets of beliefs mentioned above. It becomes apparent that if we believe the first view we will treat followers one way. If we believe the second view we will treat followers quite differently. Our beliefs play a vital role in determining our actions as leaders.

A Reason to Act

In a previous life as an adjunct psychology professor at a state university, I taught "Theories of Motivation." After years of study and reflection, I concluded that the idea of motivation is fairly simple—to be motivated a person needs *a reason to act*. Behavioral scientists call this a stimulus or precipitating event. Our reason to act can be simple or complicated. Sometimes the reason is external to us, for example, our car is dying, so we buy a new one. Sometimes the reason is internal, such as longing for meaning and purpose in our lives. In every case, a person's action begins with a reason to act. Our reason to act passes through a belief, which then determines the actions we take.

Our belief system is critical to our behavior. We constantly form beliefs about one thing or another, and we keep those beliefs in what we can metaphorically call a "belief file." This file, which resides in our core, catalogues our many beliefs on many different topics. Once filed away, a belief waits to be applied to a particular stimulus (e.g., the sight of a bug automatically retrieves the most relevant belief in the file, in Anne's case, "Bugs are harmful."). Figure 8 illustrates how all this works.

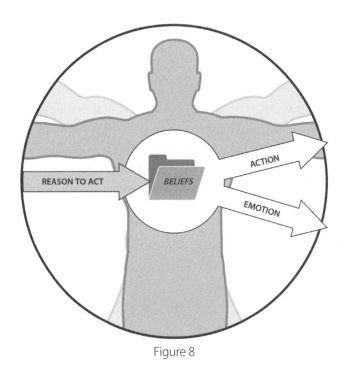

Figure 8

A reason to act passes through a belief. That belief determines our action, which results in an action or an emotion or, most likely, both. Of course, this process happens almost instantaneously, and it tends to happen unconsciously. In some cases, there are competing thoughts flying around inside our core, but we are most aware of the stimulus and our action. Because this process happens so quickly, our awareness of how a specific belief intervenes is limited to nonexistent at the time our actions occur. When Anne saw a bug, she did not stop and thoughtfully consider her belief about bugs. She just screamed and ran.

As you can imagine, not everything we believe is accurate—most bugs, for example, are not going to hurt us. If the belief governing a behavior does not accurately reflect reality, our resulting action will also be off track. Many beliefs are downright false. If an inaccurate or false belief is stored in our belief file, it will result in a misguided action.

Ideally, we make sure that our beliefs are true and grounded in reality. Because our belief file resides within our core, we must carefully guard our core to be careful about what gains access. We must thoughtfully decide which beliefs remain in our belief file as well as which presently stored beliefs need to be reconsidered or jettisoned. All kinds of influences act upon our beliefs. Not all those influences foster accurate or true beliefs, so we must learn to detect errant beliefs and to challenge their authenticity. We need a way to keep those errant beliefs out; we also need to challenge existing beliefs that may not be true.

Consumer products companies spend countless billions to influence our thinking. Those efforts are measured in terms of "impressions," and for many products, the impressions run into the millions in any given year. These marketing experts are masters at shaping our beliefs, and we act on those beliefs by buying their products. The ads are so effective that we even see them as entertainment during the Super Bowl. A battle rages 24/7 to influence our beliefs, and the other side is well-funded. Ads about perfume, razors, and cars foster beliefs that govern our behavior. There is tremendous effort on the part of many to shape not just our beliefs about consumer products, but also politics, social attitudes, and many other areas. In addition to ads, social media holds immense power to influence individual and collective beliefs. Many feel that we have only begun to see the impact of social media in shaping what people believe.

It has always been of interest to me how certain catchphrases enter our speech. If you like the media personality Larry the Cable Guy, you have probably used his catchphrase, "Git-R-Done!" In the last six months, I noticed how many people have begun to start their statements with, "So." Our high school grammar teacher would seriously frown on starting a sentence with a conjunction, but this speech pattern has worked its way into the common vernacular. Just as these popular speech patterns unconsciously work their way into our own vernacular, beliefs also work their way into our belief file.

This unconscious adoption of a speech pattern or, more important, a belief is even more likely when prominent figures who we admire espouse certain beliefs. I am surprised at how often we let others do our thinking for us. For example, a Hollywood figure supports a particular political candidate. We admire the actress, because she is brilliant on-screen. "If she is voting for this candidate, so will I" is the quiet, almost imperceptible inner dialogue. We do not stop and challenge the validity of her belief. In reality, the actress may be outstanding at her profession but have no depth of understanding in domestic or political matters. Also, her beliefs about life, personal values, faith, money, etc. may be dramatically out of step with our broader beliefs. We will unpack this phenomenon more in Chapter 12, but the key takeaway is that we must be careful to vet the beliefs that work their way into our belief file, especially the subtle ones that lodge themselves in our core with little to no conscious awareness on our parts.

ERRANT BELIEFS/ERRANT ACTIONS

Many of our beliefs are rational and well-founded, while others are not. Fairly routinely as I work in various organizations, I discover that conflict among executives is rooted in false beliefs about one another. I met with a national sales manager recently who was steaming because one of her peers was going straight to people in her part of the organization to get information. I asked the leader what about this upset her. She responded, "I don't like her going around my back, and it upsets my people that she seems to be questioning my judgment." I happened to know that the marketing manager, who was new to the organization, was actually trying not to bother the sales manager by asking every time she needed to know something to get her job done. I encouraged them to talk about the problem. The new marketing manager had come from an organization where she was expected to know everything about the product and her previous organization's culture was not to observe any organizational boundaries when asking questions. These two leaders ended up agreeing that the marketing manager, out of courtesy, would tell her peer what she needed to know and find out the best way to get it. The real breakthrough occurred when the sales manager admitted that she had attributed negative motives to the marketing manager—she owned her misbeliefs. In fact, the new manager was not questioning her judgment, but rather trying not to bother her colleague unnecessarily. The sales manager changed her belief about her new co-worker, and over the following year, their trust level grew. They now they work together famously.

A Leader Who Needed a Better Belief File

Dennis Kozlowski is now serving time for misusing company funds at Tyco International, the huge security products company. He dipped into company coffers for a lot of personal stuff; for example, he bought a $6,000 shower curtain for his Manhattan apartment.[2] He apparently had some very expensive and exotic tastes, because from my bachelor days, I remember a shower curtain costing about twenty bucks, ten for the liner and ten for the curtain, including the locking plastic rings.

How does the model in Figure 8 explain Kozlowski's behavior? Kozlowski's apartment needed a shower curtain (Reason to Act). I am only conjecturing here, but maybe he was so busy, he asked his designer to buy and install a suitable shower curtain. When Kozlowski received the bill from the designer he thought, "Wow, that's a lot of money, but I've done so much for the company over the last two years, I think the company should pay for that. I'll also probably entertain some business prospects here" (Belief file). Based upon the errant belief, he paid the bill out of the company's entertainment budget (Action).

Where did Kozlowski go wrong? His action was wrong, certainly, but the problem actually originated in his belief file. He needed a shower curtain—no problem there; however, in response to his need, his faulty belief system said, "You deserve this and shouldn't have to pay for it personally." He acted on that belief and felt good that he was not stuck with the bill out of his own pocket. The root cause of his problem was not his action but rather that a particular belief in his belief file did not reflect reality. The correct belief should have been, "This is a personal expense."

What if Kozlowski had caught himself and said, "That's a lot of money for a shower curtain. It's tempting to have the company pay for it, but there is no way ethically to justify it. I either need to pony up the money personally or ask the designer to find a less expensive shower curtain." If he had modified his belief about how the company should pay for the curtain and some other items, Kozlowski might have made a great impact at Tyco and be enjoying his retirement today.

OUR BELIEFS CAN BE INFLUENCED

An emerging leader's beliefs regarding how to treat subordinates or how to advance in the company are often like an empty file. Other people become instrumental in forming the beliefs that govern how we act as leaders. This argues for picking our role models carefully, because a given leader may powerfully impact what beliefs guide us.

I do not know what influences formed Dennis Kozlowski's beliefs. He may have had more ethically robust beliefs earlier in his career. As we observed earlier in the book, the acquisition of power can change our beliefs—power can corrupt our beliefs, which corrupts our actions. Power acts forcefully on our core. Ungoverned, it can do a number on our beliefs, twisting them into self-serving purposes. When we lie to ourselves, we create errant beliefs that we eventually adopt as true. In many cases, the adoption of these errant beliefs does not happen thoughtfully, but rather unconsciously. Consider the implications for a leader who believes, "I don't have to follow the normal rules . . . my position is above that." Leaders are especially vulnerable to this pitfall because they have more power. Power, by its very nature, potentially influences a leader to creatively engineer ways to justify their decisions even when the belief that guides their actions is errant.

Our beliefs are so controlling in their impact that they can even determine whether we live or die. Laura Hillenbrand's fine biography of Louis Zamperini, *Unbroken*, tells the gripping story of three survivors when their B-24 crashed in the Pacific Ocean during World War II. Louis Zamperini, Russell Allen Phillips ("Phil"), and Francis McNamara (Mac) struggled to stay alive for many days under a relentless tropical sun with no provisions in a flimsy raft surrounded by sharks.

Her description of their ordeal captures the power of beliefs and their impact on behavior:

> Though all three men faced the same hardship, their differing perceptions of it appeared to be shaping their fates. Louie and Phil's hope displaced their fear and inspired them to work toward their survival, and each success renewed their physical and emotional vigor. Mac's resignation seemed to paralyze him and the less he participated in their efforts to survive, the more he slipped. Though he did the least, as the days passed, it was he who faded the most. Louie and Phil's optimism, and Mac's hopelessness, were becoming self-fulfilling.[3]

Mac died quietly one night, and his two companions gave him a mournful burial at sea. He died largely because he believed his circumstances were hopeless. Louis and Phil spent forty-seven days on the ocean before the Japanese finally took them captive.

In most cases our beliefs do not determine whether we will live or die, but they will have a huge influence on whether we will be a strong leader who makes a great impact. We need to be intentional and thoughtful regarding what we believe. It is essential that we understand how certain beliefs make us effective as a leader, while others set up for cataclysmic failure.

We must be tough-minded in determining which beliefs we will allow into our belief file. Beliefs must be vetted. The ones we do not vet can get us into serious trouble. We must conduct a persistent, courageous, and introspective review if we are to access the beliefs and convictions that control our behavior as leaders. Every belief must be interrogated and put on trial for its life.

---

*Every belief must be interrogated
and put on trial for its life.*

WHAT DO WE REALLY BELIEVE?

Although we may entertain some theoretical beliefs that we share during casual conversations with friends, deep down in each of us is a set of real convictions that determine our actions and emotions—these are our core beliefs. In a great scene near the end of *Indiana Jones and the Last Crusade*,[4] Indiana Jones, his father, and a cast of evil characters converge in a cavern carved out of ancient sandstone dimly lit with smoky torches. Both groups' quests lead them to this desolate desert cave, which they believe to be the secure location of the Holy Grail. The villainous Donovan is certain that the Holy Grail is the key to eternal life and wants desperately to retrieve it for his own selfish ends. He sends a couple of soldiers into the adjacent passageway. After the vibrating metallic sound of a giant blade reverberates through the cave, two severed heads roll back to the feet of the group to a chorus of screams. Out of desperation, Donovan shoots Indiana Jones's father to force Indy to enter the lethal gauntlet of obstacles to retrieve the Grail (the only thing that can save his wounded father). With a flourish of contempt, Donovan says to Indy, "It's time to ask yourself what you believe." Indy is now forced to consider whether the search for the Grail is an archeological abstraction or a reality able to heal his father's mortal wound.

GO DEEPER

When we vet our beliefs, it's essential that we deliberately and wholeheartedly examine what we *really* believe. Too often we tend to cut ourselves a lot of slack and may not do the sort of honest self-examination that surfaces those faulty belief files.

Spend a quiet Saturday morning reflecting on your personal belief file:

1. What do you believe to be your role as a leader?
2. Examine what you believe about key figures in your life (e.g., your boss, your peers at work, etc.).
3. Identify what important beliefs you may have absorbed over time. Who influenced your adoption of those beliefs?
4. What are some beliefs you may have held at one time but later concluded them to be errant?
5. Has there ever been a time in which you sacrificed (paid a price) for an important belief you held?
6. What do you really believe about the people you lead?
7. What are some beliefs you might be harboring that could compromise your effectiveness as a leader?

The next chapter provides some insight about how we actually discover the beliefs nested in the depths of our core.

CHAPTER 9

ARE YOU TALKING TO ME?

"There's not a day goes by I don't feel regret. Not because I'm in here, or because you think I should. I look back on the way I was then, a young, stupid kid who committed that terrible crime. I want to talk to him. I want to try and talk some sense to him, tell him the way things are. But I can't. That kid's long gone and this old man is all that's left. I got to live with that."

—RED (SPEAKING TO PAROLE BOARD AT THE
PRISON WHERE HE SERVED A FORTY-YEAR
SENTENCE), *SHAWSHANK REDEMPTION*

My wife once had a several-months-long conversation with herself about a bowl. She owns an art gallery on a street known for fine antiques stores and other galleries. On the way into work one day she stopped by one of her favorite stores to look around and noticed a beautiful green bowl on a shelf with some other accessories. The bowl seemed to call out to her. The depth of the color and the beauty of its workmanship seemed almost otherworldly. The store owner said he thought the bowl was probably from China. Anne could not take her eyes off it, and every instinct in her said to buy this bowl. She then looked at the price—$1,000!

"Wow, that's a lot for a bowl that is just going to catch dust on a shelf," she said to herself. "Also, there's no way I can hide that much money from

Tim in our budget. I'd better not." She went on to work but could not stop thinking about the green Chinese bowl. She returned to the store the next day, and said to herself, "I really should buy this," but then she decided, "No, I'd better wait."

Three weeks later, Anne went back to the store, and the bowl was marked down to $600. The bowl possessed an eerie but beautiful patina. A glow emanated from somewhere deep within its contours. Anne had never felt drawn to an object like this, and her mind returned to the bowl countless times during the day. She wrestled within her soul. One side spoke to her saying, "Buy the bowl." The other side said, "Six hundred dollars is still too much money."

The "Buy the bowl" side finally won out, and she went to the store the next day. It was gone! The store owner said a man came in right after her the day before and bought the bowl.

Several months later, Anne again stopped by the antiques store. The owner said, "Anne, you won't believe this. The guy who bought the Chinese bowl took it to the antiquities department of some university for evaluation. It's more than three thousand years old, and they conservatively estimate it is worth $300,000! University archeologists speculated that it was a burial urn for some emperor."

I told Anne that if she ever has a similar experience to please listen to herself sooner and buy the bowl! Anne's only consolation is that now the bowl is in a museum and can be enjoyed for what it is. We would have probably used it to hold paper clips on Anne's desk.

ARE YOU HEARING VOICES?

When I speak to groups of leaders I often ask them if they talk to themselves. There is usually a nervous ripple of laughter, and a few brave souls raise their hands. We may not acknowledge it or even be aware of it, but the truth is we all talk to ourselves.

Self-talk is the often haphazard and sometimes directed flow of thoughts, ideas, and feelings that course through our core. The conversation

We may not acknowledge it or even be aware of it, but the truth is we all talk to ourselves.

is inside me, not between another person and me. Self-talk is our intrapersonal, not interpersonal, communication. This is analogous to our use of an intranet to share internal documents inside a company, while the Internet allows us to communicate outside the walls of our organization. Each of us has a constant flow of self-talk going on inside us most of the time. Psalm 16 says, "Even at night my [core] instructs me."

Sometimes our self-talk is dialogue; sometimes it is even a debate. Sometimes we question ourselves, "Should I do this or not," as in the case of Anne trying to decide whether or not to buy the bowl. In these situations, we often experience what psychologists call cognitive dissonance (basically, internal emotional discord). Part of me wants to do something, and the other part of me puts on the brakes. Our self-talk expresses the battle that rages between the conflicting sides.

Some self-talk is affirming, as in, "I felt good about how I led the meeting today." At other times we are giving ourselves a stern lecture, like, "Don't you ever do that again." This critical style of self-talk often resembles the voice of a parent or grandparent who may have been a bit crotchety. Sometimes we speak to ourselves in the first person, such as when we chide ourselves: "I'm so stupid. I can't believe I did that." We might yell at ourselves, or our self-talk can be a quiet whisper that only the most careful, intentional effort can discern.

We talk to ourselves—that is clear. The question is, "Are we listening?" Under the right conditions, we can actually listen to this inner dialogue, regardless of the decibel level. In fact, I believe we *must* learn to listen in. Paying attention to our inner voice can be extraordinarily helpful, and a failure to do so may put our ability to lead in grave peril. The key is not just hearing but, when necessary, learning to forcefully change the message of our inner voice to be a strong leader.

WHAT DOES SELF-TALK TELL US ANYWAY?

Self-talk reveals the narrative of who you are as a person. Author Patrick Rothfuss said, "It's like everyone tells a story about themselves inside their own head. Always. All the time. That story makes you what you are. We build ourselves out of that story."[1] Although self-talk may seem random, we are constantly building and revising our own narrative inside our core. In my experience, most people are quite passive about their narrative. Their narrative is formed in pinball fashion, where they bounce from one person and experience to the next. They give little effort to self-authoring a story about where they want their lives to go and the legacy they want to live. Their narrative is formed through the collective wisdom of *Entertainment Tonight* and *People* magazine.

By contrast effective leaders are thoughtful about who they are and where their lives are going—the narrative they are creating. For example, they are often contemplative about their values—those pivotal priorities that guide their lives and actions as leaders. We have a good sense about these leaders—we call them "highly principled" and we follow with abandon. They inevitably make an impact.

LISTEN TO YOUR CORE

There are three particularly important aspects of our self-talk. First, self-talk originates in our core—yes, our cores talk! Self-talk is the pipeline to our core, and it flows in two directions. We can hear our core speak to us, and we can speak to ourselves. For many of us, our core is strange and inaccessible. The thought that a person is actually talking deep down inside of us is a bit spooky.

Second, what we say to ourselves has a profound impact on our behavior because it feeds our beliefs. Our self-talk not only reveals our existing beliefs, but also, we can speak to our core to thoughtfully form or change our beliefs. If we repeatedly tell ourselves that we are stupid, we will believe it. Imagine the feelings and actions that flow from that belief. I do not know about you, but I want to know what those beliefs governing my behavior are. If we learn to monitor our self-talk, we can control our beliefs and the resulting behaviors.

Third, self-talk can be full of surprises, because it taps into the hidden area of the awareness circle, the model shown in Chapter 4. Listening to self-talk is one key way we get inside the hidden area. In a conversation with the CEO of a company, I asked him why he was so down on a particular manager. He recoiled from my question and said, "What do you mean down on?" I told him that every time I heard the manager's name mentioned in the CEO's presence, he frowned. A couple of weeks later we talked again, and he said, "I found out what the problem is. In the first week after he joined us, 'Joe' said something about our company's reputation in the marketplace that I took very personally. I've never gotten over it. Last Saturday morning I was doing some preparation for the week ahead and actually heard myself say, 'That guy can't be trusted.' He's really a stellar performer. I didn't think I doubted Joe's loyalty, but that first impression created a doubt in my mind that stuck for three years. I need to change what I believe about him. He is a good guy whom I love having on the team. I hope the frown is gone."

HOW DOES IT WORK?

Listening to our self-talk requires that we get in position to hear. Self-talk is easily crowded out by the noise in our lives. Electronic distractions need to be turned off and set aside. You cannot usually hear your self-talk while answering an e-mail or watching the news. Listening requires undivided attention.

One of my favorite forms of exercise is biking in the North Georgia mountains. Because there is so little traffic where I ride, I hear my inner voice more clearly than usual. I am always surprised at how much verbal traffic is going on in my head. I try to pay attention and very often get new ideas about how to handle a particular interaction or what to write.

One way I hear my self-talk is by sitting in a very quiet place and thinking about my day ahead. I try to spend a few minutes with a calendar and journal in front of me. I reflect on what I think and feel about the people and events on my calendar. When I listen carefully, I discover beliefs about people that will guide my behavior toward them.

One practice I have found to be helpful during this morning period of reflection is to "move toward the resistance." If I do not want to do something or think about something, it is probably a subject I should actually spend some time considering—move toward the resistance and figure out what the resistance means. Not long ago, as I looked at a person's name on that day's calendar, I heard myself say, "Cancel the meeting with him." As I took a few minutes and asked myself why, I realized that the person with whom I had a meeting that day often has a hidden agenda and wants me to agree with him about the faults of another colleague. I actually do not like meeting with him and find that it is difficult to have a clean, unencumbered conversation with this person. I did not cancel the meeting but decided in advance that we would stay on task. That one small awareness was helpful in guiding my behavior during our meeting.

Speaking to Our Core

Listening to our self-talk is vital, but remember that the communication also needs to go the other way. I worked with a leader in the fashion industry who was renowned for draining all the energy in meetings. Some committee or group would ask her to attend and report on her initiative that had an impact on their work in some significant way. What she failed to see was that the groups who invited her to their meetings wanted a dialogue. Instead of a five-minute update, she inevitably gave a forty-five-minute lecture on her project and its merits. Repeatedly, I heard frustration around the organization about her boring monologues.

I sat down with her one morning and talked about what I was hearing. She responded by pointing out that "Others said they wanted a report, and I am simply responding to their request." I said, "Rather than seeing this as a report, why don't you think of this as an opportunity to engage them and to build support for your initiative. They're telling you they want to hear from you, but what they really want is to interact with you. Let them do most of the talking." My feedback challenged a firmly held conviction in her belief file.

She said, "This is a pretty ingrained practice for me. How do I change it?"

"Talk to yourself."

She responded, "What?"

"Before you meet with a group the next time, tell *yourself* that what you're really after is to get them on your side. Tell *yourself* that the only way you're going to get them on your side is to get them involved. Tell *them* that you would be happy to answer their questions, but that you really want to hear from them, where they are having hiccups with the process, etcetera."

"Okay, I'll try that," she said.

The next meeting was a huge success. The group did most of the talking and became a champion of her initiative. She got the point. She changed her belief about the purpose of her meetings, and her behavior changed—as did the results.

Apart from having a conversation with herself, the executive in this example would still be giving her forty-five-minute monologues, because that is what she genuinely believed people wanted. Her belief was errant, and she had to talk to herself to change that belief. We must learn to proactively talk to ourselves.

SELF-DECEPTION IS INDEED DECEIVING

Self-deception is explored more fully in the next chapter, but here is the basic idea. It is not news that we sometimes lie to ourselves. Yes, and often our core protests—there goes that cognitive dissonance again. Lying to ourselves can easily result in errant beliefs. For example, if a leader says to herself, "I don't have to follow the normal rules," and fails to capture and alter this misguided belief, she will be in grave peril. Errant behavior flows from errant beliefs.

Errant behavior flows from errant beliefs.

I worked with a client organization that was, how can I say this nicely, frugal. Actually, by most people's standards, the leaders were downright cheap. They asked me and two or three of my team members to participate in a meeting at a particular hotel near an airport three to four times a year. I did not like the hotel. It seemed unsafe and had a reputation for unsavory characters. The hotel staff was unprofessional. Despite my misgivings for the team and me, I kept my opinions to myself, and we continued working at the hotel. I told myself to be a good team player and serve the client.

One morning I arrived for an early meeting, and the front desk clerk gave me a key to the meeting room so I could get set up. I inserted the magnetic key card into the lock and opened the door. Just enough light came in through the open door to make me realize that the room was occupied by another guest. I am still amazed at how quickly this happened, but all of a sudden a man who looked like a character straight out of *Breaking Bad* sat up in bed and pointed a huge handgun at me. I apologized for the mistake and quickly closed the door. I then went back to the desk clerk and quietly asked for a new room (actually I wasn't that quiet).

That afternoon, driving home, from out of nowhere I literally screamed, "I will never under any circumstance go back to that hotel!" The strength of my feeling shocked me. It was just plain stupid to have meetings there. My core had been quietly telling me for a long time to request that we meet in a better hotel—"You are putting yourself and your team at great risk," my core had told me—but I had ignored the message under the pretense of false humility. I lied to myself that we were "trying to serve our customer." Self-deception had gotten the best of me. Later that week, the client and I had a candid conversation, and we changed hotels for future meetings.

Listening to our core is a critical discipline for a leader who makes an impact. This prevents us from taking the path where, like Red in the opening quote of this chapter, we lament the loss of the legacy that could have been. In the next chapter, we will look at some fairly predictable ways we can lie to ourselves to achieve likewise fairly predictable results.

GO DEEPER

Spend twenty to thirty minutes in a quiet place listening to your self-talk—eliminate the noise around you. Write down what you're hearing and answer the questions below. Do not worry about the somewhat random style of your inner communication.

1. What are the messages you hear from your core?
2. What does your self-talk tell you about the life narrative that you are creating?
3. What are your most significant apprehensions about your effectiveness as a leader?
4. What do you need to say to your core about those apprehensions?
5. Do you notice any self-talk that may not be objectively true?
6. Does your self-talk reveal anything that puts you at risk personally and as a leader?
7. Do you find yourself resisting reflection on some topic? Do you push toward that subject and ask yourself why you find that topic difficult?

Make it a regular practice to listen to your self-talk throughout the day. The next subject is the type of self-talk that really gets leaders in trouble. We must pay great attention to our potential self-deception.

CHAPTER 10

LIES LEADERS LOVE

"Man is not a rational animal, he is a rationalizing animal."

—ROBERT HEINLEIN

A few years ago, I worked with a manufacturing organization that was redesigning its main operating processes. The CEO asked me to facilitate a meeting where a number of different leaders in the company would be discussing how their respective parts of the process could dovetail once implemented. The event was in a beautiful old hotel with lots of mahogany trim and old oriental rugs. Within a few minutes of checking in, I was hanging up my clothes and heard a voice coming through the back wall of the closet. The occupant in the room next door was on a cell phone talking loudly. The walls of the old place were so thin, it was like this person was standing in my room. I made a conscious effort not to eavesdrop, but even humming the *1812 Overture* really loudly did not help. What was worse, I knew exactly who the person was. Even worse than that was that it was very obvious who was on the other end of the call and what they were talking about. It was not company business. Two senior officers of the company, one of whom reported to the other, were having a torrid affair. I knew one was married and had several children. I knew the other was recently divorced. A few months later a janitor discovered the pair in his office after hours in a very compromising position. The senior executive was fired, and the company settled what could have been a nasty sexual harassment suit.

I have not seen either party since they left the company, but I would love to interview them to find out what they were thinking. What were they telling themselves about the affair? How did they justify the relationship that had so many pitfalls and conflicts?

SELF-DECEPTION: WE DECEIVE OURSELVES

Although some might maintain that these two people were not thinking at all, my experience as a psychologist tells me that their belief systems underwent some significant reformatting in order to justify their actions. We can only speculate about what their distorted belief file might have been. The most troubling explanation would be that one of them promoted the other and believed there should be something in return. Both might have believed that "This is just a physical relationship and is not hurting anyone." It might have been that "Lots of people in the company have slept around; it's not a big deal." What if they believed they were deeply in love but needed some time to work out the complexities? Even in a culture in which moral relativism is in fashion, we probably agree that their actions were wrong. Whatever tortured logic they might have applied to justify their behavior was simply self-deception: "The act or an instance of deceiving oneself, especially as to the true nature of one's feelings or motives."[1]

> **Self-deception:** The act or an instance of deceiving oneself, especially as to the true nature of one's feelings or motives.

In self-deception, we choose to believe that something is true when, in fact, it is *not* true in order to bring about a state of inner harmony. We insert a different belief into our belief file that provides us with personal harmony instead of the discordance we may feel about our actions or prospective actions. Why would we do this? The simple answer is that we have the innate ability to choose a belief that makes us feel better about ourselves and/or less guilty about something we are doing. We are capable of muting that unpleasant accusation we feel when there is something we really want to do. This self-trickery allows us to do what we want and feel less discord than when we deliberately violate what we know is right.

Self-deception can be so misleading that even when individuals for whom we have great respect tell us we are going off track, we deny the basis for their concern or ignore their advice entirely. Powerful individuals can even start to believe they are invincible. *Game Change*, John Heilemann and Mark Halperin's book about the 2008 presidential campaign, documents the repeated efforts by many senior members of John Edwards's political party to persuade him to abandon his sexual misconduct with a campaign staff member. Edwards either denied his affair with Rielle Hunter or ignored their advice.[2] His downfall became inevitable and imminent because of his self-deception.

WHAT MAKES LEADERS VULNERABLE TO SELF-DECEPTION?

As mentioned in Chapter 6, it is often power in some form (organizational position, wealth, fame, etc.) that breaches the containment walls of our core and makes us more vulnerable to self-deception. Power not thoughtfully regulated weakens our core, causing the inner person of the leader to become less able and/or less inclined to challenge errant beliefs.

Dennis Kozlowski and his shower curtain mentioned in Chapter 8 provide some important insight about how power weakens the walls of our core. We can only speculate, but his self-deception might have gone something like, "I made Tyco what it is today . . . I deserve this . . . the shareholders owe it to me . . . I am entitled to a few perks." Although the shower curtain and the many other excesses in which he indulged strain credulity for any rational person standing off to the side, a leader intoxicated with power and success actually believes the lie and then acts on it. Self-deception invariably sets the stage for the lapses in judgment that Kozlowski clearly had.

How Do We Deceive Ourselves?

In the news conference where Tiger Woods apologized for his extra-marital affairs, he illustrated how self-deception occurs. "I knew that my actions were wrong, but *I convinced myself that normal rules didn't apply*" (italics mine). By adopting a false belief we act in a way that, in a rational moment, may seem absolutely crazy. Given that Tiger Woods was violating his marriage commitment, he may have said to himself something like, "I deserve this. I am rich and famous. I have a stress-filled job and am gone from home much of the year. The normal rules just don't apply." By inserting this belief into his belief file, Tiger, at least temporarily, reduced the disharmony he felt over what he was doing.

When contemplating a certain action, we can "believe" ourselves into behaviors that put us and others in great jeopardy. Tiger's "new belief" was not true, and eventually, his self-deception caught up with him. Later, in the same news conference quoted above, he admitted his self-deception. "I was wrong. I was foolish. I don't get to play by different rules. The same boundaries that apply to everyone apply to me."[3]

Power also potentially makes us narcissistic. At the same news conference during which Tiger Woods discussed his marital infidelities, he admitted that "I never thought about who I was hurting. Instead, I thought only about myself."[4] Narcissism makes us more prone to find beliefs that justify our actions even though those actions are uniquely self-serving and may even cause harm to others.

When we choose to change our beliefs, we do not have a rousing epiphany, and say, "I think I'll change my belief so that I'll feel better about myself." Rather, this debate happens at the level of our quiet inner voice. This is why self-talk is so important. Unless we pay attention, the belief change occurs with little to no self-awareness. The re-engineering of our beliefs is usually subtle, not blatant, because it occurs over time deep within our core.

Once established in our core, false beliefs then get us off track. We simply lie to ourselves via a false belief (self-deception), then talk ourselves into doing something wrong, risky, or just plain dumb. We act even at the risk of self-destruction.

The dominos of flawed beliefs begin to fall. We lie to ourselves. We buy the lie as truth. We then sincerely tell others the "truth" that we have convinced ourselves is true. We will never forget President Clinton staring straight into the camera to assure us that "I did not have sexual relations with that woman, Ms. Lewinsky." Somewhere inside Clinton's twisted logic, I think he actually believed what he was saying. We have an unlimited capacity to rationalize our behavior, and self-deception is in its most powerful state when we believe the lie ourselves. Leaders who lie to others lie to themselves first.

TEN LIES LEADERS LOVE

In past research I learned that for those leaders whose cores were compromised in some significant fashion, self-deception was always present. It became clear that there is at least one lie in there somewhere. Although self-deception can take many forms, there seem to be some more frequently occurring and predictable "lies" to which leaders succumb. The following are ten familiar self-deceptions—lies to carefully avoid:

1. "I'm the smartest person in the room. I have better ideas and better judgment than anyone on the team."

2. "I'm responsible for these results. They could not have done this without me. I did this."

3. "Everyone is out to get me because they are envious. I am so good, and they can't stand it. They know I'm on the fast track and are going to try to get me off track."

4. "These people work for me. They have to deliver to my standards. I need them to focus on helping me."

5. "I don't have to follow the normal rules . . . I deserve special consideration. I have a big job and need to ignore some rules to get my goals accomplished."

6. "I'm entitled to that. I worked hard and made this place what it is. This place was a wreck before I took over. Through my leadership we are finally making some money."

7. "It's not material. This is a rounding error. No one would begrudge me for taking this."

8. "No one will ever know. We can fudge these numbers a little. Next quarter should be spectacular, and we can restate this quarter's earnings."

9. "It's not my fault. I did everything I was supposed to. Those other guys dropped the ball."

10. "I don't need to be accountable to anyone. Nobody here really understands what I'm trying to do. It's only results that the board is after, and I can get those if the rest of the team would get out of the way."

We might be saying at this point, "I would never entertain the above ten statements even for a minute." Before we write off the personal relevance of the above list, be aware that these lies come in many differ forms creatively crafted to support the actions we want to justify.

Are we less vulnerable? In actuality, no. Many people who derail in leadership positions have similar backgrounds to us. They worked hard to get ahead. They sacrificed to go to school. They overcame limitations in their background. They became emotionally resilient through stress and difficult decisions. They were successful and gradually given more and more leadership responsibility. Absent the diligent guarding of our core, their story could easily become ours.

SELF-DECEPTION BREAKS US

Several years ago I was alone on a Friday night while Anne visited her mother. I started channel surfing and randomly landed on the movie *Unthinkable*, which tells a very disturbing story about a subterranean government agent who tortures people during national security crises to get critical information. Samuel L. Jackson plays "H," the shadowy figure who uses horrific, unthinkable interrogation methods to save the country from 9/11-type attacks. The movie raises all kinds of legal and moral issues, but what I found most interesting was H's statement, "Every man, no matter how strong he is, lies to himself about something. I will find your lie. I will break you."[5]

"Every man, no matter how strong he is, lies to himself about something. I will find your lie. I will break you."

—"H" IN *UNTHINKABLE*

The more obvious symptoms in someone who falls from a position of influence are arrogance, narcissism, fear, lack of authenticity, or a failure of self-regulation. Underneath these symptoms are false beliefs similar to those Tiger expressed in his news conference—"I don't have to follow the normal rules" or "I'm entitled," etc. I have heard people say, "Tiger got caught, and that's the only reason he apologized." I do not know if that is true, but isn't it amazing how many people do get caught? General David Petraeus is thought by many to be the smartest and most competent general to lead the U.S. military since World War II, and yet he lost his job as director of the CIA over a tabloid affair. Self-deception has a way of breaking us no matter who we are and how buttoned-up we might be.

Maybe we do not personally identify with the list of ten lies in the "Ten Lies Leaders Love" box; however, there is a high degree of likelihood that we lie to ourselves about something equally consequential. This lie becomes our Achilles' heel. The pressure of more responsibility, more power, or more visibility inevitably puts us at greater risk for self-deception if we are not careful. Self-examination and the resulting self-awareness are not frivolous exercises. Effective introspection thoughtfully catches us in the act of self-deception and corrects our own belief system before the lie breaks us.

It is important to clarify that I am not saying we are bad people. It is highly unlikely that we are latent ax murderers. What I am saying is that we have vulnerabilities that must be understood and addressed if we want to be leaders who make an impact with our lives. Great leaders are desperately needed today, but our world is filled with challenges, pressures, and stresses that make it difficult for us to sustain an enduring legacy.

Tell Ourselves the Truth

Kenneth Lay, former CEO of Enron, along with a few other insiders, agreed to misstate quarterly earnings.[6] Misstating earnings is a go-to-jail offense, which is where Lay would likely be today if he had survived a heart attack in his Colorado vacation home. Lay's close associate, Jeffrey Skilling, went to jail to serve a twenty-four-year sentence.[7]

I did not know Kenneth Lay, but his personal story is fairly typical of many leaders. He grew up in meager circumstances. He studied hard, received a Ph.D. in economics, and served in the U.S. Navy. He shrewdly navigated the founding and growth of a major company in the energy business. He gave a lot of money to charitable causes and was a committed member of his church. Many who knew him well would say he was a good man.[8]

Enron was a fast-growth company that wowed everyone with its market dominance and meteoric rise in value. There was tremendous pressure to maintain the value of the stock. The pressure was so intense that even a good man for very good reasons would seek any way to keep the company's stock performing well.

We can only speculate about what Lay might have said to himself, but it likely went something like this:

> I just told all the employees to invest their 401(k)s in our stock. If we report poor earnings, the market will kill us, and a lot of our really good people will lose money and their excitement about our company. My credibility will be shredded. We're going to get earnings back on track. These accounting maneuvers are aggressive but will keep our stock price up. We will get the profits up and do a restatement of earnings for this quarter sometime later this year.

What if Ken Lay actually said something to himself like I described above? What if he had caught himself in the lie that in essence said, "The end justifies the means." What if he had challenged that belief and said, "We cannot and will not misstate Enron's earnings because that is inconsistent with my own and our company's values. That would be a fundamental violation of our company's core value of integrity." This is all a matter of speculation, but it is plausible that Enron would still exist and be a thriving contributor in the energy world, and that any losses in Enron's stock value would have eventually recovered—if only Ken Lay had arrested his false belief.

The most important point to capture here is that we are just as vulnerable as Ken Lay or any other fallen leader if we do not apply certain disciplines to protect our core. How we catch ourselves early in the process of self-deception and change those errant beliefs is the subject of the next chapter.

GO DEEPER

Look at the list "Ten Lies Leaders Love" and assess your vulnerability to each self-deception:

1. "I'm the smartest person in the room. I have better ideas and better judgment than anyone on the team."

1	2	3	4	5
Not at All Descriptive		Sometimes Descriptive		Highly Descriptive

2. "I'm responsible for these results. They could not have done this without me. I did this."

1	2	3	4	5
Not at All Descriptive		Sometimes Descriptive		Highly Descriptive

3. "Everyone is out to get me because they are envious. I am so good, and they can't stand it. They know I'm on the fast track and are going to try to get me off track."

1	2	3	4	5
Not at All Descriptive		Sometimes Descriptive		Highly Descriptive

4. "These people work for me. They have to deliver to my standards. I need them to focus on helping me."

1	2	3	4	5
Not at All Descriptive		Sometimes Descriptive		Highly Descriptive

5. "I don't have to follow the normal rules ... I deserve special consideration. I have a big job and need to ignore some rules to get my goals accomplished."

1	2	3	4	5
Not at All Descriptive		Sometimes Descriptive		Highly Descriptive

6. "I'm entitled to that. I worked hard and made this place what it is. This place was a wreck before I took over. Through my leadership we are finally making some money."

1	2	3	4	5
Not at All Descriptive		Sometimes Descriptive		Highly Descriptive

7. "It's not material. This is a rounding error. No one would begrudge me for taking this."

1	2	3	4	5
Not at All Descriptive		Sometimes Descriptive		Highly Descriptive

8. "No one will ever know. We can fudge these numbers a little. Next quarter should be spectacular, and we can restate this quarter's earnings."

1	2	3	4	5
Not at All Descriptive		Sometimes Descriptive		Highly Descriptive

9. "It's not my fault. I did everything I was supposed to. Those other guys dropped the ball."

1	2	3	4	5
Not at All Descriptive		Sometimes Descriptive		Highly Descriptive

10. "I don't need to be accountable to anyone. Nobody here really understands what I'm trying to do. It's only results that the board is after, and I can get those if the rest of the team would get out of the way."

1	2	3	4	5
Not at All Descriptive		Sometimes Descriptive		Highly Descriptive

From the above list, which lies are you most vulnerable to lodge in your belief file?

CHAPTER 11

OUR BELIEFS ABOUT OURSELVES AND THOSE WE LEAD

"Non sibi sed patriae." Not self but country.[1]

—UNOFFICIAL MOTTO OF THE U.S. NAVY

Before I met Anne, she moved to Washington State from Wisconsin after a job transfer. Anne's roommate, Donna, drove with her to help with the long trip, which was made a bit more difficult because they were towing a U-Haul trailer with all of Anne's earthly possessions. When they reached the top of the Continental Divide, it was Anne's turn to drive, so they stopped briefly to enjoy the sights. The beauty of the pristine snow against a piercing blue sky, the crisp air, and the dramatic vistas of the Rocky Mountains renewed their spirits after many hours on the road.

After traveling a few hundred yards down the steep grade of the western slope, the trailer began to rock violently, pushing the car from side to side. Other cars traveling in both directions tried to move out of the way of what appeared to be a catastrophic accident in the making. Anne fought unsuccessfully to control the car, the tires squealing as the trailer tossed the car in every direction. Just as Anne started to step on the brakes,

Donna screamed, "Anne, don't step on the brakes, step on the gas!" Anne later said that accelerating the car went against every instinct—she wanted the car to slow down before they experienced a catastrophic accident. She yielded to Donna's plea, and within a few seconds of stepping on the gas, the trailer settled down and began to roll smoothly behind the car.

Anne explained that the steep downhill grade made her drive tentatively. Gravity took over and the heavy trailer began to move faster than the car. It quickly stepped out of its rightful position as a "follower" and began an attempt to pass the car with nearly disastrous results. Stepping on the gas caused the car to pull the trailer as intended, but Anne had to speed up to get the car to move ahead and reassert its position as the "leader."

ENGAGING THE COMMITMENT OF FOLLOWERS

Without leadership most human endeavors would never get off the ground, much less prosper. Organizations today face some of the most difficult conditions imaginable. The turbulence index is off the charts, and news reports warn of a new impending disaster every day. Now is the time for leaders to lead. Leaders are understandably uncertain and tentative about the economy and market conditions, and they often must lead a workforce with its own unrest. In these circumstances, leaders must step on the gas. Perhaps as never before, they must get out in front to garner the hearts and minds of followers. Although accomplishing the task is imperative, leaders particularly need the commitment and resourcefulness that only engaged followers possess.

As we discussed in Chapter 1, Colonel Joshua Lawrence Chamberlain faced his own crisis on the outskirts of Gettysburg in 1863. Chamberlain instinctively knew that he could not *command* the men to follow and fight with courage and sacrifice. He believed the mutineers would join in only if they were reminded of the importance of their cause and shown the personal meaning of their military service. Chamberlain's beliefs informed his words, and the soldiers willingly followed him into the battle that determined the course of the war.

What a leader believes about those he or she leads plays a dominant role in whether or not the heart and minds of followers are engaged. When we hear what Chamberlain said to the mutineers, it becomes apparent that he believed most of them desired to serve a higher end. Chamberlain believed that all men have value and that residing within each mutineer was a noble self who recognized that inherent value as well. He believed that reminding these men about the noble purpose of the war would engage their hearts and minds, so that they would unreservedly join in the effort. During his short speech to the mutineers that so dramatically changed their perspective, Chamberlain said:

> This is a different kind of army. If you look at history you'll see men fight for pay, or women, or some other kind of loot. They fight for land, or because a king makes them, or just because they like killing. But we're here for something new. This has not happened much, in the history of the world: We are an army out to set other men free. America should be free ground, all of it, from here to the Pacific Ocean. No man has to bow, no man born to royalty. Here we judge you by what you do, not by who your father was. Here you can be something. Here is the place to build a home. But it's not the land. There's always more land. It's the idea that we all have value, you and me. What we're fighting for, in the end . . . we're fighting for each other . . .[2]

At this moment, the mutineers' hardened resistance softened, and all but four joined in the effort to defeat the Confederate Army in the pivotal battle. This was not a management technique but rather an authentic action that flowed out of Chamberlain's core. He believed in the inherent noble motives of his followers, and that when presented with the opportunity, they would make the right decision. To use a modern term, he *empowered* them to determine their own destiny. He spoke from his core to their core, and they were transformed. They re-enlisted with personal commitment to a high calling.

Many leaders today take the path of pragmatism—they are impatient and bottom-line oriented. They approach the task with expediency only to discover, at the end, that no one is following them (like Doug Dennison in the Prologue). Some leaders complain that what I am suggesting is too time consuming. "We just need to get the job done." They discover that the long way, counterintuitively, is the short way. When we lead effectively, we ensure that the work is completed well, but we also gain the commitment of followers to willingly exceed the basic requirements of their jobs. The ability to engage people in this deeper way flows from an intact core.

INTENTIONALLY DETERMINE OUR LEADERSHIP PHILOSOPHY

Our leadership philosophy is a belief system, and therefore it guides how we act as leaders. Earlier in the book I stressed that beliefs govern our behavior. Nowhere is this more powerfully manifested than in what we believe about people, our role as a leader, and the work we do. As with others we must vet these beliefs and root out any that are fundamentally untrue.

How we act depends on what we believe about people and their trustworthiness to do their jobs. A somewhat extreme but entertaining example is Captain Bligh in the original screen version of *Mutiny on the Bounty*. In one memorable scene the captain tells his younger officers about how to motivate "half-witted seamen" on a ship. "Now don't mistake me. I'm not advising cruelty or brutality with no purpose. My point is that cruelty with purpose is not cruelty—it's efficiency . . ."[3] As a consequence of his leadership philosophy, a number of Captain Bligh's crew chose mutiny.

Our beliefs about people, about work, and about ourselves determine what kind of leader we become and the depth of commitment of our followers. We should be intentional and thoughtful about what we believe about human nature in general and about our followers in particular.

Followers still commit mutiny today—it is called not following the leader's vision. As mentioned earlier, Bob Nardelli, the failed CEO of Home Depot who liked his private elevator, so alienated the members of the organization that they refused to follow his vision. This became obvious to Home Depot's board, and the board removed him from leadership.

WHAT DO WE BELIEVE ABOUT PEOPLE?

A much more contemporary maritime epic, *Crimson Tide*, reveals major differences in what two men believe about their crew. Gene Hackman's character, Captain Ramsey, and Denzel Washington's character, Commander Hunter, trade barbs over how to lead the crew of their submarine during a nuclear standoff with Russia.

> HUNTER: Captain, here's the results from the missile drill.
>
> CAPT. RAMSEY: [looks at the missile drill results] Is this the best they can do?
>
> HUNTER: No, sir, but that's what they did.
>
> CAPT. RAMSEY: I want this down to five minutes. Train on it.
>
> HUNTER: Yes, sir.
>
> CAPT. RAMSEY: Tell your buddy Weps to do it again, and keep on doing it until he gets it right.
>
> HUNTER: Yes, sir.
>
> CAPT. RAMSEY: It looks like the whole crew needs a kick in the ass.
>
> HUNTER: Or a pat on the back, sir. I witnessed a fight down in crew's mess—no big deal. It appears that the crew is a bit on edge about all we're going through. Morale seems a bit low.
>
> CAPT. RAMSEY: [picks up the intercom and speaks into it] May I have your attention please, crew of the *Alabama*. Mr. Hunter has brought it to my attention that morale maybe a bit low, and you might be a bit . . .

[looks to Hunter]

HUNTER: [whispers] On edge.

CAPT. RAMSEY: [over the intercom] On edge. So, I suggest this. Any crew member who thinks that they can't handle the situation, can leave the ship right now. Gentlemen, we are at DEFCON 3, war is imminent. This is the captain. That is all.

[hangs up the intercom]

HUNTER: Very inspiring, sir.[4]

[Hunter's statement drips with sarcasm]

Ramsey's harshness makes it apparent that he believes he must diminish the crew to achieve the boat's mission and to get the results he seeks. Hunter believes they will get more out of their crew through defusing the high tension levels and encouraging the crew. We can argue on either side of this divide, but it is essential that we wrestle with the question, "How do I move followers from a state of compliance to a state of commitment?" Whether in a war, business, or a nonprofit, we want to ensure the followers' engagement in unrestrained pursuit of the mission.

WHAT DO WE BELIEVE ABOUT OUR ROLE AS LEADERS?

Effective leadership can be summarized by a simple, time-tested equation:

$$Q \times A = E$$

The quality (Q) of an idea times the acceptance level of followers (A) equals the effectiveness (E) or actual results from the idea.

Many leaders focus on the task and build high levels of quality into their initiatives. No one could fault this emphasis. What they may neglect is how well their initiative will be accepted by those it impacts. Using a simple one-to-ten scale for Q and A: A ten idea times a zero-acceptance level equals zero effectiveness.[5]

This model should govern the role and priorities of a leader. If a leader believes his role is to design organizational systems to ensure the quality of the products, his focus will be on engineering the product or service and then designing metrics to monitor the product quality. The leadership equation above, however, suggests that the leader must place at least as much emphasis on engaging the hearts and minds of those who must own and implement the idea. No matter how profoundly good the idea, a follower's willing endorsement of the idea and its means of implementation are also foundational to the leader's role. We saw the lack of attention to employee acceptance illustrated in the fictional example in the Prologue of this book.

I consulted with a manufacturing plant that was part of a huge multinational corporation for several years. The company's market share of the products produced in the plant was dropping like a rock due to cheaper foreign imports. The plant manager asked me to help redesign the work to meet the joint goals of higher quality and lower price. Though the plant manager initially resisted my idea, I strongly recommended she include several members of the local union on the design team. There were some brutal conflicts, but we persisted until we were convinced that we had the right answer for the redesign. In one of the first redesign sessions, the plant manager introduced the central concept for the redesign that was eventually adopted and implemented. Six months later during the all-employee presentation, one of the union representatives took credit for originating the plant manager's idea. He actually presented the central tenet of the redesign as if he had come up with the thought himself. He told the members of the union why it was such a good idea and why he expected them to embrace it enthusiastically. His involvement in the process engaged him so fully and his acceptance level was so high that the idea became a part of his DNA. The plant manager and I had a good laugh privately. She shrugged and said, "Who cares who gets credit for the idea as long as this works."

Many great initiatives go down in flames because the leader did not seek to involve the consumers of the idea or those who would be responsible for its implementation. Inherent in the model are several foundational beliefs. The model says that it is not enough to have a really well-engineered product or service. It suggests that followers will do a better job if they buy into an idea. It assumes that followers' ownership of an initiative is important to the quality of outcome. Not every leader believes this, but the evidence about how followers excel in the twenty-first century argues strongly for the accuracy of the model. Any leader will want to examine and challenge his or her belief file on this point.

It's All about Me

I routinely hear leaders say, "He works for me." This is a literally true statement if we look at the org chart; however, what do we *really* believe? Are my followers working to make me successful or am I seeking to ensure my followers' success? Some leaders see their team as a resource to accomplish *their* job.

An alternative view is that our job as a leader is to set overall direction and then to make sure the team has the knowledge, skills, and resources necessary to make good decisions and to accomplish its goals. As leaders, our job is to secure what they need for success. Our job is also to work outside the team to build alignment with other leaders and to remove roadblocks to the team's progress. We coach them through problems and monitor key metrics to make sure we keep our commitments to other parts of the organization and to our external customers.

Leaders believe something, and our behavior as leaders (how we see our own role and how we treat our followers) will manifest those beliefs. Introjection is "a mental mechanism in which the standards and values of other persons or groups are unconsciously and symbolically taken within oneself."[6] We sometimes learn how to lead by how we are led. If we unquestioningly introject our beliefs about people and our role as leaders, we risk the adoption of some views that are simply not true. Thoughtful examination and testing of what we believe remains critical to sustaining great leadership.

Introjection is "a mental mechanism in which the standards and values of other persons or groups are unconsciously and symbolically taken within oneself."

LEADERS POINT TO MEANING

Great leaders engage the hearts and minds of followers and use the meaning of the work to achieve this. When people are paid fairly, they will work harder for meaning than they will for money. The catch is that if we do not see the work as noble, it will be hard to convince others that there is meaning to the job.

Someone might well say, "Look, we make cardboard boxes. We are not freeing people from slavery. I'm not sure I can appeal to my team members' sense of nobility. How do I engage them over something so common as a box?"

The answer may lie in talking with the team about why what they are doing is important. Why is it important that the quality of those boxes be outstanding? What is shipped in those boxes that makes people healthier, safer, smarter, better looking, or happier? Maybe that box is holding someone's dream. Most people are doing jobs that have meaning whether or not they have considered it. People want to feel they are doing something meaningful. Going to work is a lot more fulfilling when we make a connection between what we do all day and how we help others. A leader's role is to help make that connection. Getting line of sight to the end user often helps create that meaning.

Bringing Out the Best

Leadership is a critical role in every dimension of life. Our beliefs have a huge bearing on whether we succeed in not only getting the task accomplished, but also in truly bringing out the best in the followers we serve. Most leaders tell me that they believe the members of their organizations are capable of performing at a higher level than they presently are. My response is, if they are capable, then why are they not performing at that level? Leading from an intact core is the foundation from which exceptional performance is possible. That intact core guides how we treat followers and how we invest time not only in the product quality but also in the quality of our team's engagement.

Over the course of this book, I have talked about a wide range of disciplines tied to strong leaders who sustain that leadership over a long period of time. It is an intact core that ultimately makes this possible.

GO DEEPER

Situations and people vary, but what do you believe to be true about the people you lead? Here are some options. Please place a check on the spectrum below in the box that reflects what you *really* believe about followers. They:

1. Do the minimum necessary to keep their jobs.

1	2	3	4	5
Seldom the case		Sometimes the case		Almost always the case

2. Need to be controlled and directed to accomplish the organization's goals.

1	2	3	4	5
Seldom the case		Sometimes the case		Almost always the case

3. Need stern consequences if they fail to perform.

1	2	3	4	5
Seldom the case		Sometimes the case		Almost always the case

4. Need attractive incentives to perform well.

1	2	3	4	5
Seldom the case		Sometimes the case		Almost always the case

5. Want to excel and do quality work.

1	2	3	4	5
Seldom the case		Sometimes the case		Almost always the case

6. Are fundamentally lazy.

1	2	3	4	5
Seldom the case		Sometimes the case		Almost always the case

7. Are fundamentally hard working.

1	2	3	4	5
Seldom the case		Sometimes the case		Almost always the case

8. Are self-motivated.

1	2	3	4	5
Seldom the case		Sometimes the case		Almost always the case

9. Do mainly what they are told.

1	2	3	4	5
Seldom the case		Sometimes the case		Almost always the case

10. Work for money.

1	2	3	4	5
Seldom the case		Sometimes the case		Almost always the case

11. Work for meaning.

1	2	3	4	5
Seldom the case		Sometimes the case		Almost always the case

12. Care only for themselves.

1	2	3	4	5
Seldom the case		Sometimes the case		Almost always the case

13. Care about the customer.

1	2	3	4	5
Seldom the case		Sometimes the case		Almost always the case

14. Care about co-followers.

1	2	3	4	5
Seldom the case		Sometimes the case		Almost always the case

15. Are noble, well-intentioned, and want to do what is right.

1	2	3	4	5
Seldom the case		Sometimes the case		Almost always the case

16. Want to add value to their work.

1	2	3	4	5
Seldom the case		Sometimes the case		Almost always the case

Our fundamental beliefs determine how we lead. Our beliefs about people reside in our core and must be thoughtfully examined and challenged when necessary. Obviously people vary, and we can think of examples of people who fit each of the statements above. Look back over your list and ask yourself:

1. What are the likely consequences of the beliefs that I hold about followers?
2. Are these beliefs about followers going to make me a great leader?
3. What beliefs must I question and possibly change?

CHAPTER 12

DETONATE
FALSE BELIEFS

"Jerry, just remember, it's not a lie if you believe it."

—GEORGE COSTANZA

Anne has been in the art business for many years and represents about thirty artists whose works are on display in her gallery. After I arrived home from work one afternoon, a friend called and said, "Is that Anne's gallery on channel five? The sky copter is looking down on her store." I had no idea what she meant and quickly switched on the TV. There was her store's awning with Anne Irwin Fine Art emblazoned on the front. Just as the sound and image came on the screen, the TV announcer reported, "We have a bomb threat at Anne Irwin Fine Art in Buckhead. Numerous law enforcement agencies are on the scene."

My jaw dropped. Just as I turned to run to my car, Anne called. "We're all fine, but every law enforcement known to man is here—the Atlanta Police, the Atlanta Bomb Squad, Homeland Security, and the FBI to name a few. The street is closed and no one is allowed to enter or to leave the area. Now was the first time they would let me call you! I hope you will come down, but you may not be allowed on the street."

Fortunately, when I arrived, I was able to park nearby and walk to where Anne was standing on the sidewalk. It was bedlam. Several sky copters hovered overhead. Ten police cars were parked in haphazard fashion around the street with blue lights flashing, and a specially equipped ambulance waited nearby. Fire trucks with red lights flashing and firefighters were everywhere, and their water hoses crisscrossed the street. A gigantic bomb squad truck waited near the gallery entrance and a mechanical robot stood at attention on the sidewalk.

Visibly shaken, Anne showed me a photo on her phone of a box that had been delivered to the gallery earlier that afternoon. The major delivery services routinely deliver and pick up art all day long, but this box arrived from a well-known fashion retailer. Anne's gallery manager had ordered a purse for her sister's birthday. When she removed the purse, she saw that underneath were three long tubes with something white on the inside. Wires connected the white tubes to some kind of digital control panel. Anne took one look and called the police, who arrived within minutes. The police examined the box and quickly backed away, telling everyone to clear the building.

The head of the bomb squad explained to Anne that for safety reasons they routinely detonate anything that looks like a bomb in a special water tank on the truck. The robot carried the package to the truck, placed it in the tank, and blew it up. The tank is so well fortified that they can conduct carefully controlled detonations of even significant bombs. They then attempt to reassemble the device to understand its true nature. This is a painstaking effort that the "lab guys" undertake to determine the type of explosive and its origin. How did the detonator work? Was it an amateur effort or more advanced in its design?

A variety of officials interviewed Anne and her gallery manager. "Did they have any enemies? Was anyone recently fired from the company?" No one had any explanation, and no one from any of the agencies was talking. A few days later, a Homeland Security official stopped by and reported that they had concluded the package had nothing to do with the gallery. The experts were not even positive it was an improvised explosive device, although everyone agreed it looked like one. They speculated that terrorists may have been testing the package delivery system, but otherwise the authorities were very tight-lipped. Anne took some comfort from the fact that everyone with whom she dealt in the law enforcement community was incredibly competent, concerned, and highly professional.

HAVE YOU EVER THOUGHT ABOUT THE WAY YOU THINK?

In the last chapter we looked at the consequences of false beliefs and self-deception. It is quite normal to hold beliefs that are completely false or even just half-truths. These misbeliefs result in actions that are ineffective at a minimum, and in some cases downright dangerous. Most leaders with a breached core have lied to themselves about something. The issue for us is how do we identify those misleading beliefs, and then what do we do about them.

In the case of Anne's gallery, the authorities from the Atlanta Bomb Squad were able to execute a controlled detonation to deal with the device safely. When we discover false beliefs in our core, we, too, must find a way to bring about a controlled dismantling of that belief so that it does not influence our behavior in a harmful direction. It is also a useful exercise to consider how we adopted the false belief in the first place.

Recently, I was trying to get home from a trip to attend a wedding party for a friend. The gate agent told me that my flight was cancelled due to a mechanical problem in Atlanta. He said he would get me on the next flight an hour-and-a-half later. Although it is a bit embarrassing to admit this, I experienced a torrent of negative self-talk.

> That gate agent is lying like a dog. That's such a lame excuse. They just didn't have a full load, so they're saying it's a mechanical problem, when they just don't want to fly a half-empty plane up here. He's crazy if he thinks we're only going to be delayed ninety minutes. I'll get into town just in time for Friday afternoon rush-hour traffic. Anne and I will have to race back across town in traffic to get to the party. We'll be incredibly late. I'll go to bed at a ridiculous hour and won't get to do some critical things I've got to get done early in the morning.

My first impulse was to complain to the agent and say a few unedifying things, but instead I sat in the gate area and sulked for about fifteen minutes, replaying the same catastrophic sequence over and over, feeling sorry for myself. This was a really great response for an experienced organizational psychologist who writes books about how to be an effective leader!

What were the beliefs that were in play? One belief was that airlines don't tell the truth and do not care about inconveniencing their passengers. A second belief was that I would be very late, and there would be all kinds of negative consequences.

Fortunately, I remembered that I was writing this book and began to have a different conversation with myself. The first thing I said was, "This is something I cannot control. Even if the airline is lying about the reason for the flight cancellation, the gate agent, the pilots, and the flight attendants had nothing to do with that decision. There's no sense in being annoyed with them. There is really no way to confirm the reasons for the flight cancellation anyway." I also did the math on the time: "I may hit some rush-hour traffic, but even in worst-case scenario, we probably won't be more than thirty minutes late for the party. I can also get some calls made and e-mails sent while I'm sitting here at the gate."

I felt a bit better and actually got some work done. Hopefully, I added a few hours to my life by not going into an artery-clogging negative emotional spiral! The good news is that my re-engineered self-talk proved to be about right and we were not that late for the party.

EXPLODE FALSE BELIEFS

My flight example above is trivial compared with the beliefs that get us in real trouble and compromise our ability to lead, but the process for how we identify and arrest those false beliefs is pretty much the same. If we listen carefully to our self-talk, we can often ascertain our beliefs. To listen carefully, we have to be quiet and eliminate as much of the noise as possible. Even though I was at a noisy airport in my previous story, I was able to find a seat in an empty section of chairs. This helped me close out some of the distractions and be reflective. The end goal is a controlled demolition of false beliefs. In many cases we can simply identify and then challenge or dispute the false beliefs heard in our own inner dialogue. We can then replace those false beliefs with ones that are true.

The process looks like this:

1. Ask, "What am I telling myself?"
2. Determine what belief(s) your self-talk reveals.
3. Consider the behavioral consequences of that particular belief—what are your resulting conduct and feelings?
4. Ask yourself, "Are these beliefs true? Which beliefs need to be disputed and changed?"
5. Conduct a controlled detonation of the false beliefs—tell yourself that these beliefs are simply not true.
6. Tell yourself the truth and put those new beliefs into your core.
7. Finally, act on the basis of the new beliefs.

WE ARE COMPLICATED

This short seven-step process is not as easy as it might seem. Our behavior is often highly nuanced. We have strongly ingrained beliefs that do not disappear at the flip of a switch. We tend to be skilled at engineering our beliefs to be compatible with what we really want, and those beliefs become well-defended.

Our misbeliefs are not always easy to identify, particularly when there may be some half-truths present. Those half-truths can be as hard to spot as a sniper in camos hidden in natural terrain. The especially challenging aspect of a half-truth is there is likely some truth in there somewhere—just distorted. Ken Lay's half-truth was based upon the conviction that "We have to take care of our stockholders, many of whom are employees with their entire nest eggs tied up in Enron stock." That part was a true statement and very good camouflage for the lie that followed: "We will get our books in order next quarter."

Although some problems, like my bad attitude at the airport, may be resolved quickly, our more enduring patterns and habits require heightened vigilance and determined perseverance to change. It is good to cure ourselves of annoyances over routine inconveniences like late flights, but there are far more consequential issues we must address. As leaders, we can impact thousands of lives, as Lay did at Enron. Effective leaders must be ruthlessly intolerant of any self-deception.

How Does This Work?

Let's look at one of the Lies Leaders Love from Chapter 10: "I'm the smartest person in the room." You just might be the smartest person in the room. Maybe you went to a prestigious university and graduated with honors. Maybe you worked for a prominent firm before going to a top-ten business school. Maybe you did not even finish college, but like Bill Gates, you are known as a brilliant person who has a tremendous ability to keep multiple ideas in play at the same time. Maybe you have been involved in some spectacular successes at your company and everyone sees you becoming the CEO in seven or eight years. Maybe you are the CEO. Even if these statements are true, here are some dangerous self-deceptions that may flow out of a foundational belief like "I'm the smartest person in the room":

- I am more important than everyone else.
- I have the keenest insight and know better than others.
- The company should implement my ideas without question.
- Although there are some good "doers" on this team, I am the best "thinker."
- My judgment about most matters is superior to others.

The behavior we would likely observe in the person who holds these types of beliefs would include dismissiveness, arrogance, impatience, and diminishment of others, to name a few. As the person is given more responsibility and power in the organization, he or she tends to give even fuller expression to these qualities. The self-talk of someone whose beliefs are like those above might sound like:

> Well, I have to sit through another tedious leadership team planning meeting today . . . these things are boring and nothing but a pooling of ignorance. I told them three months ago what we should do, and now we're about to conclude that's exactly what we will do. When I get the top job we're going to dispense with these time-wasters.

Although others may respect the person's brilliance, they are not going to follow an arrogant person wholeheartedly. They are not going to invest in that leader's vision and will find themselves subtly resisting and maybe even sabotaging the leader's initiatives.

Effective leaders pay attention to their self-talk. They challenge those subtle misbeliefs and half-truths that they carry around in their core. They recognize that a certain tone or gesture conveys arrogance or dismissiveness. They recognize that this type of behavior breeds resistance to our ideas in others.

We must challenge and reject some of our long-held beliefs and substitute new ones such as:

- Every member of this team has an important role and a valuable contribution to make.
- I have good insights but different perspectives tell the whole story.
- Many of my ideas are insightful, but sometimes I don't have all the facts.
- An effective team will always outperform any group of individuals.
- The team values my judgment, but I must offer my insights with humility and deference to be well-received.
- I may not have all the facts, so my ideas need to be challenged.

As we go through this process, we must remain vigilant in self-examination. We must ask others for feedback. We must deal sometimes forcefully with our belief system and speak directly to our core with conviction, saying, "I must stop viewing others as inferior and start affirming their unique perspectives." When we hear one of those false beliefs creeping back in, we can say, "Stop . . . . that is not true. Although I do have a significant talent, others are uniquely gifted as well."

EARLY-WARNING SYSTEM

Having an early-warning system can keep false beliefs from lodging in our core. Senator John Edwards had a plethora of early warnings from others, but he ignored them. He either insisted that he was not having an affair or he promised he would stop. It is now public knowledge that Edwards had the affair and fathered a love child with his mistress. He survived a civil trial in which he was charged with misusing campaign funds to pay her.[1] Although we do not know what types of alarm bells might have been going off inside his core, there were bound to be some present. Ignoring the early-warning system left his campaign and his life in shambles.

Whether the early-warning signals come from inside or outside, we need to learn to heed them. Misbeliefs can be sticky and hard to dislodge over time. They become familiar and well-practiced. It would be like getting rid of an old friend. In some instances, we must draw on the resources of others such as an accountability relationship—the subject of an upcoming chapter.

I worked with a senior manager who was a perfectionist. No one liked working for her. Meetings meant obsessing over the smallest details. She displayed self-righteous glee when she found mistakes in others' work. Her peers called her a "sick puppy." The CEO of the company told me that earlier in her career, she had been coached countless times to ratchet down the obsessiveness and perfectionism but had ignored the advice. Although talented and smart, she exercised an excessive attention to detail that made her a micromanager. Over time, her style and conduct became career limiting. She and I had lunch one day, and I asked her where her attention to detail came from. She said, "Someone who does not seek perfection in all they do is not a good person." When I asked her where that perspective came from, she attributed it to her deceased father, a highly regarded actuary who worked at the same company years before. I left lunch convinced that her views had the strength of moral conviction and was immovably lodged in her belief system. Six months later, the company downsized, and, with strong urging, she took early retirement.

Although there are many background factors that strongly influence our beliefs, I firmly believe that we do not have to live under the determination of what we learned earlier in our lives, as did the woman in my illustration above. We can certainly achieve escape velocity from any belief no matter how strongly entrenched it might be.

GO DEEPER

Ask yourself these questions, which will help you identify misbeliefs before they become too lodged in your belief file:

1. Is what I'm telling myself objectively true?
2. What is the source of my belief—is there anyone's "voiceprint" on my self-talk, like a parent or former boss? Do I really want to emulate that person?
3. What are the behaviors that flow out of this belief? Are these behaviors getting good results? Are the results sustainable? Are my followers growing and getting better at their jobs?
4. What would my most-respected mentor say about my belief?
5. If I am really honest with myself, is there any self-deception going on that provides air cover for something I basically want to do regardless? Am I being realistic about the consequences if I persist?
6. Am I lying to myself about anything?
7. Use your "phone a friend" option. If you were to call a respected peer and say, "I'm thinking about doing _____. What do you

think?" (Sometimes just considering calling a friend is enough to convince you that you do not want to do _____.)

Essentially we must ask, "Are we telling ourselves the truth?" We must ask if the narrative revealed in our self-talk is who we really want to become—our legacy. How we ensure that the right beliefs are fully lived out in our behavior is the topic of the next chapter.

CHAPTER 13

Running Me Inc.

"I keep a close watch on this heart of mine.
I keep my eyes wide open all the time.
I keep the ends out for the tie that binds.
Because you're mine, I walk the line."

—JOHNNY CASH, "I WALK THE LINE"

Several years ago I worked with the leadership team at a company whose headquarters was located in a rural area. One of the strongly held values of the company was community service, and the CEO encouraged employees to be involved in their town. Several of the senior officers regularly volunteered as chaplains at a nearby federal prison. During one of my visits to the company, the executives who volunteered at the prison asked me to attend a session with a group of inmates with whom they met several evenings a month. I gladly accepted their invitation. After a group session, a number of the prisoners came up to have individual conversations with me. A few shared their personal stories. One of the most poignant stories I heard that night was from a man who had served about half his sentence.

"Joe" told me that he was a highly recruited high school basketball player. He was so good, some had speculated he might go straight to the NBA; however, his parents insisted he first go to college. He had scholarship offers from a number of Division I university basketball programs all over the country, and had accepted an offer at a well-known basketball powerhouse not too far from his home. After high school graduation, Joe said good-bye to his coaches and friends and spent the summer working out and taking a math course to get ready for college. Just like his dad, Joe wanted to major in business. One night a friend invited him to a bar. Although he was underage, his friend assured him that it did not matter. They drank a couple of beers and then headed for the door. Joe wore a T-shirt for his college team, and as they were leaving, another guy at the bar made an insulting comment about the basketball team. Ignoring him, Joe kept walking, but then the guy grabbed him from behind. Joe reacted quickly, swung around, and hit the other guy squarely in the head. The other man dropped to the floor and died instantly. A jury found Joe guilty of manslaughter, and the judge imposed the mandatory minimum sentence of twenty-five years in a federal prison. One man dead and the extraordinary promise and potential of a young life extinguished in a microsecond.

This story is tragic on so many levels. Despite the hardening that twelve years of prison would produce in anyone, Joe still had the joy of the game in his eyes, but he also exuded learned helplessness, the blight of many in such circumstances. Joe said he did not even think about his action at the time. When the guy grabbed his shoulder and said, "I'm talking to you," he simply reacted.

Although we cannot understand what it is like to be Joe, we all act on impulse at times. In a leadership team meeting I saw a young executive push back against a proposed organizational structure that the new CEO said she was considering for their company. To everyone's surprise, he blurted out, "You're wrong." I honestly do not think there was much if any forethought given before the young executive made the comment. He may have been fully justified in his concern and courageous to express it, but his timing was terrible—it was the first meeting for the CEO with her new team. The member of the team who spoke out had no relational history and, metaphorically speaking, no deposits in the CEO's trust account. A few months later the CEO asked her outspoken team member to leave the company. This story did not get reported on *Fox Business*, but the executive suffered a permanent loss of credibility and his position.

Like Joe and this uncensored team member, many of us act or speak without deliberation, contemplation, or forethought. We just act or speak. We sometimes regret things that we say in meetings and wish we had caught ourselves before the fateful words rolled out. "Why didn't I just sit back, not say anything, and see where the discussion was going? But no, I had to jump in and now look like a moron." An ancient king known for his wisdom said, "Fools vent their anger, but the wise quietly hold it back."[1] The good news is that effective self-regulation frees us from the tyranny of our impulses.

[E]ffective self-regulation frees us from
the tyranny of our impulses.

TWO MARSHMALLOWS ARE BETTER THAN ONE

Walter Mischel, a former Stanford professor of psychology, performed one of my favorite research studies. Young children sat in a room with an experimenter and were offered a deal. They could eat one marshmallow now, but if they waited until the experimenter left the room and then returned in fifteen minutes, the child could have two marshmallows. Many of the children showed no restraint and ate the marshmallow immediately. Others waited and were awarded a second marshmallow. Mischel pointed out that the children who waited for the second marshmallow often managed their impulses by distracting themselves, for example, looking at something different. The children with the ability to self-regulate were strikingly different from the immediate gratification group when the children were studied again ten and fifteen years later. The ones who were able to delay gratification scored much higher on a number of measures, for example, social adjustment and SAT scores. The low-delay group had more behavioral problems at home and at school. "We can't control the world," Mischel observed, "but we can control how we think about it."[2]

ARE WE ACCOUNTABLE FOR OUR REACTIONS?

A lack of self-regulation is at the center of many leader failures. Failure to regulate behavior inevitably undermines a leader's aspirations to be strong and to have an enduring legacy.

Earlier in the book, I mentioned General David Petraeus, head of the CIA, who was forced to resign over an extramarital affair with his biographer, Paula Broadwell. What was he telling himself about his relationship with Ms. Broadwell? We do not know. This is only conjecture, but it could have been along the lines of, "She is an extraordinarily accomplished and beautiful woman, and she's fun to be with. I am really lonely because of the travel and demands of my job. She respects me for who I am. This is not hurting anyone. We won't get caught." One of the truly outstanding generals in U.S. history compromised his legacy by allowing self-deception to prevail in his core. When there is a breach in a leader's core, there is a lie in there somewhere!

Could General Petraeus have resisted the affair with Broadwell? We cannot control the events or temptations coming our way, but we can control our thinking. Paula Broadwell *is* a beautiful and accomplished woman. That indisputable reality General Petraeus could not control, but strong leaders have moments of truth where they must regulate their actions. Contemplation of an inappropriate relationship with a subordinate or using company resources to buy something for personal use or a million other possibilities should provoke a self-awareness moment.

What Petraeus could control were his beliefs about Broadwell and their relationship. Effective self-regulation involves having tough-minded, candid, and forceful conversations with ourselves to challenge the misbeliefs. What if the general had said to himself:

> She is an extraordinarily accomplished and beautiful woman, and she's fun to be with. I am really lonely because of the travel and demands of my job. She respects me for who I am. It is incredibly tempting to go the next step with her, but I must not. Even though it's been fairly common for men in my position to have affairs, the

potential devastation to our families, our reputations, our careers, and maybe even national security are at stake. I must create some strong safeguards immediately to limit any further involvement with her.

Changing our beliefs to regulate what we are doing or contemplating doing often requires a self-induced wake-up call. It is like that foggy state between wakefulness and dreaming, when we start to realize the dream is not reality. We say to ourselves, "This was just a dream." In that foggy state between contemplation of an action and the action, we have to speak directly to our core. It requires intense monitoring and managing of our beliefs—making sure that what we are telling ourselves is true.

Could Joe have "coached himself" out of the spot he was in at the bar? Probably, but it would have required that he draw on some belief he already had nurtured in his core. Most athletes have to develop self-control to stay in the game, or at a minimum, to not get penalized or ejected. During intense competitive events, many athletes lose composure and shove or hit an opposing player; however, the best athletes learn restraint. Their self-talk says, "Don't react. You will hurt the team if you take out your frustration this way."

We might think that we "just reacted—things happened so fast," and we couldn't help it; but, in reality, there is always a belief in there somewhere that directs our actions. Joe might have felt insecure in the bar because he believed it to be a dangerous, threatening place. He might have been on edge because he believed he would get in trouble with his strict parents for drinking. He might have believed the only way out was physical confrontation—that he simply could not walk away because of ego reasons. I cannot say what he believed, but what appeared to be an impulsive, senseless act actually came out of a flawed belief. His unsound decision about how to handle the situation bore that out.

Most people who regret impulsive acts or decisions actually had restraining self-talk going on during their misguided action, but the stress and noise of their circumstances drowned out their quiet voice of reason. The executive I mentioned earlier in this chapter reacted because the proposed new organizational structure diminished his position and created another reporting level above him. He was flooded with feelings of concern that he and his team would lose standing in the organization, which is why he blurted out, "This won't work." With enough presence of mind, he still should have said to himself, "Sit on this. Build a relationship with her and then state your case when she knows that you support her in the position."

It takes time and discipline to self-regulate, but it is not enslaving. In fact, it is the opposite. Self-regulation frees us from the tyranny of our impulses. Self-regulation is like the pressure regulator in my home. For some reason unknown to me, the water pressure is excessively high on the street where my home is. To address this, a plumber installed a pressure regulator in my basement, near where the water supply pipe enters from the street. The regulator controls and reduces the pressure so that our appliances and plumbing fixtures are not damaged. In the same way, we need a personal regulator that governs what we do and say, so that any excessive pressure or stress does not damage critical relationships and our credibility as leaders. So how do we create such a regulator inside us?

High School Biology

I am reaching way back, but I recall from high school biology that a semipermeable membrane is a barrier that allows certain substances to pass through while blocking others. A membrane of this type serves as a protective mechanism. We need a personal semipermeable membrane around our belief file, so that we are very selective about what we allow through and what we block out. Figure 13 illustrates this how this works.

Leaders need to be especially careful about the beliefs they allow to lodge in their belief file. We must also carefully examine the ongoing conversation we have with ourselves that reveals the beliefs we have already passed through the membrane. Periodically re-vetting our exiting beliefs is a healthy, regular exercise. We must take ourselves in hand to ensure that the beliefs we allow entrance to our belief file are true.

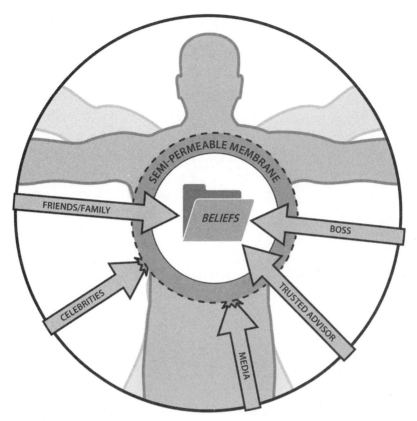

Figure 13

As we have seen in so many examples mentioned earlier in the book, power and arrogance erode our core and weaken our ability to make good judgments about what is true. The more power we acquire as we move up through the ranks of our organization, the more careful we must be to protect our core from the Lies Leaders Love.

Sometimes we have to speak forcefully to ourselves to overcome the "noise" around us. We have to be thoughtful about flawed cultural norms that we unconsciously absorb. We live in a *Jersey Shore*/Kim Kardashian reality TV culture, where some role models of behavior are absurdly flawed. Reality shows may be entertaining in a mindless way, but by any standard of behavior, do we want to live like these people? The risk emanates not from wanting to be like these twenty-first-century jesters, but rather from the subtle influence on our personal beliefs. When we find ourselves using TV entertainment figures as moral plumb lines such as the hapless monk in the cartoon below, we are in trouble.

Although many influences seem absolutely harmless on the surface, they actually have great power to shape our beliefs. Whatever we allow to go into our core unfiltered and unthinking is a cause for concern. Friends know that I really like movies, but I make a conscious effort to think about the message of any movie I see. What are the beliefs the movie espouses, and do I agree? What are the messages the producer, director, and screenwriter want me to hear?

"I pick up most of my wisdom from celebrity interviews."

Media exerts a powerful, often unconscious effect on our belief systems, and leaders are not immune to these cultural influences. Because the actors in movies are usually attractive, competent, and cool, we naturally want to be like them. At some level, who does not want to be like James Bond? Have we ever rooted for the bad guy? Of course we have. They may be ruthless killers who have killed and maimed countless good people, but the power of the visual narrative can have an impact on our beliefs in some elusive way. Although we are not gunning down innocents, we may inadvertently absorb a belief in a subtle tenant of moral relativism that gets played out in our actions in totally unexpected ways.

Movies and other media often portray the beauty, freedom, and joy of infidelity. When I watched a news report of a broken Paula Broadwell and her husband carrying their children to a waiting car in Charlotte, North Carolina, this incredibly gifted leader did not look all that beautiful, free, and joyful. I wondered about what sort of legacy she has now lost.

In the marshmallow study described in the sidebar of this chapter, Mischel said the most interesting group he studied were the children who demonstrated no ability to retrain their impulses but who later became very accomplished. It offers great hope to us who at times may have exercised poor judgment. We, too, can grow in our ability to self-regulate.

In many respects, self-regulation is simply a convergence of all the disciplines that we have talked about up until this point in the book. For example, intentional introspection and self-awareness lead to self-regulation. One way that strong leaders buttress their ability to manage themselves involves being highly accountable to others for their behavior. This powerful tool is the subject of the next chapter.

GO DEEPER

It is vital that we are careful about what influences we allow to get through the protective membrane into our core. For example, we might enjoy a particular actor on screen but need to be careful about adopting his political or religious beliefs. The following is a short checklist of influences to which we could be unthinkingly susceptible. Check the box next to any influence you must be exceptionally careful to guard against:

Media

- ☐ Celebrities
- ☐ Newscasters
- ☐ Movies
- ☐ TV
- ☐ Actors
- ☐ Radio Commentators
- ☐ Political Spin Spokespeople

Authority Figures

- ☐ Leaders who are viewed as successful in the world of work
- ☐ Professors
- ☐ Knowledge Experts
- ☐ Authors
- ☐ Celebrity Experts such as Oprah or Dr. Phil

Superiors

- ☐ Boss
- ☐ Board Members

Peers

- ☐ Team Members
- ☐ Colleagues at Work
- ☐ Friends

To the side of any checked items above, list examples of any beliefs from those sources that especially need vetting. Identify examples of ideas that need to be detonated and discarded.

CHAPTER 14

WHO'S WATCHING YOUR BACK?

"As iron sharpens iron,
so a friend sharpens a friend."[1]

—ANCIENT PROVERB

One spring break vacation our family visited the Grand Canyon and rode mules down to the base of the canyon and back up the next day. Our guide cautioned us in advance that the mules preferred to walk right on the outer edge of the trail. Most of the time this was not a big deal, but occasionally the trail dropped off precipitously. Despite every effort to guide my mule to the center of the trail, "Jack" stubbornly insisted on staying near the edge. During one terrifying moment, Jack defied his sure-footed reputation. As he meandered too close to the edge, loose dirt gave way under his back feet. He slipped off the edge and barely avoided tumbling into the abyss with me aboard. Once righted, Jack continued to walk on the edge. (For the record, he now lives in a retirement community pasture for mules, and other than an occasional twitch, I have recovered from our near-death experience.)

Mules are not the only ones who walk too close to the edge. Some leaders suffer the same plight, but they are not as nimble as Jack in recovering their balance. When they slip, they often go down, sometimes taking others with them. The leader's reputation is destroyed, and the organization's brand is tarnished. Employees, stockholders, and vendors suffer. Despite the plethora of failing leaders around us, others stubbornly continue their walk on the edge, mistakenly believing their sure-footedness will keep them out of trouble.

Throughout my career as an organizational psychologist, I have seen a dramatic increase in the call for metrics and performance accountability. Organizations and their leaders face ever-growing calls to be accountable for their activities and results. Leaders are expected to be fully transparent about their financial results, and the U.S. government has passed a vast array of new laws aimed at policing corporate behavior. Boards of directors are expected to hold senior management accountable, and shareholders sometimes sue boards for their failure to fulfill this duty.

The topic of accountability usually focuses on the work of the organization. Are leaders and various units of their respective organizations accomplishing goals and achieving results determined to be important? This is accountability for the *task*, and most organizations have become fairly adept at designing goals and metrics to monitor and measure these types of results. Accountability for tasks, like our sales numbers, usually happens routinely and visibly throughout the year. Only in rare cases like Enron are there actual attempts to obfuscate results in order to intentionally mislead shareholders, boards, employees, stock analysts, and various legal authorities.

A huge dilemma is that both leaders and boards of directors struggle to hold leaders accountable for *personal behavior*. This is particularly true in the case of leaders who manage the tasks and achieve results effectively. Although accomplishing goals and achieving financial results are essential, the evidence clearly points to the failed personal behavior of leaders as being far more likely to cause a crisis in organizational confidence. This is why personal accountability is an essential discipline for guarding our core.

Recently I met with Steve Reinemund, former chairman and CEO of PepsiCo, to discuss the topic of personal accountability. Currently Dean of the Business School and Professor of Leadership and Strategy at Wake Forest University, Steve is one of the most highly regarded corporate leaders in the world.*

In our wide-ranging conversation, Steve and I discussed both the *task* and *personal behavior* dimensions of accountability, but focused more on the latter because of the subject of this book.

WHAT IS ACCOUNTABILITY?

Steve defined accountability as "Being responsible to some other person or organization for the activities and actions that we take. It is critical to an individual's performance and an organization's integrity and credibility."

Steve added that, "A good organization where high-performing people want to work is a place where people have responsibilities and accountabilities for their actions and how they perform in their jobs. High-performing organizations do a great job of defining accountability and then measuring it and holding people accountable for results on a real-time basis." He continued, "Some of the best organizations that I

---

* Steve Reinemund is currently at Wake Forest University in the role of dean of the business school and professor of leadership and strategy. A twenty-three-year PepsiCo. Inc., veteran, he led the corporation as chairman of the board and chief executive officer, beginning in 2001; he retired as CEO in October 2006 and chairman of the board in May 2007. During his time at the helm, PepsiCo's revenues increased by more than $9 billion, net income increased by 70 percent, earnings per share increased by 80 percent, its annual dividend doubled, and the company's market capitalization surpassed $100 billion. In addition to the growth of the company, Steve's legacy includes a commitment to health and wellness, diversity and inclusion, and values-based leadership. He serves as a member of the board of directors of American Express, ExxonMobil, Walmart, and Marriott. From 2005 to 2007, Steve was chairman of the National Minority Supplier Development Council. He served on the National Advisory Board of the Salvation Army from 1990 to 1999, and he was chairman of this board from 1996 to 1999. Steve also served on the board of The National Council of La Raza from 1992 to 2001 and was chairman of its Corporate Board of Advisors from 1992 to 1996. He is a graduate of the U.S. Naval Academy and served in the U.S. Marines before attending the Darden School of Business at the University of Virginia.

have seen are very clear and very specific about those accountabilities. If people join an organization and don't recognize its culture of accountability, they join at their own peril."

How Do We Make Accountability Work?

In my consulting experience I have observed that accountability does not seem to work all that well within a lot of organizations, and so I asked Steve why this is the case. He responded, "The biggest challenge of an organization is to be consistent in its definition of what is expected and in its actions. In most organizations, you can find in some form a document that lists responsibilities, accountabilities, and actions. The key is . . . are they consistently applied? When they are not, then they may as well not exist at all."

In Chapter 6 we talked about how power has great potential to erode a leader's core. As chairman and CEO of one of the largest companies in the world, Steve had immense power. I wanted to know how he kept the power, the accomplishments, and the accolades from eroding his core and how accountability played a role in that.

"I would be the first one to say that I don't think I did it perfectly," he said. "I worked at it. It was something that was important to me, and it was something that I was conscious of throughout my career . . . so many leaders have failed in this area. On one hand I was very clear in my own mind about the importance, but on the other hand, like most of us, I struggled with it. The more success you have the more chance you have to fall prey to power."

Steve explained that, "When you grow in responsibility, it is also less likely that people are going to push back on you and challenge you. You are less likely to listen. I have seen so many great leaders fall from power because they did not have others around them who would speak to them candidly.

"My attempts to be accountable included getting commitments from other people to be responsible to push back and to challenge me on a regular basis. Their willingness to challenge me helped create the environment that prevented the abuse of power. It does not always work, but it helps. I also created a 'personal board of directors,' who, like any good board of directors, provided a balance to my power."

Steve added, "I also learned from my sister and my mother early in life to think ahead and to prepare yourself for the kind of situations in which you may find yourself. When you are in those situations, you want to be able to quickly determine true north. It has been my observation that the biggest failures—moral failures, character failures, integrity failures, power failures—are not the ones that people contemplate and think through deliberately.

"The biggest challenges to our integrity are the ones that happen spontaneously and we must react quickly. A bad decision is one that can be fatal. Those are the actions that I have seen that bring most leaders down."

Steve stressed that it is critical that we prepare for the unexpected. "Early in my career, I worked for Marriott Corporation. There was a rule that only one person spoke for the company, and that was Bill Marriott. One day I spoke on behalf of the company and was quoted in the newspaper. Bill Marriott called me and let me know that was not acceptable. I was asked to go to 'media school.' As I turned the corner to go into the building where the training was to be held, there were three obnoxious reporters who put their microphones in my face and started asking me all kinds of crazy questions. They were obviously not real reporters but were part of the media training. After they exposed themselves for who they really were, we went inside and I had to watch the painful film of how poorly I reacted.

"I try to keep that visual image of being prepared in mind, not for reporters per se, but being prepared in life. When we turn that corner and something happens we are not expecting, how are we going to react? On what basis would I make decisions—moral decisions, power decisions—when confronted with the unexpected? What is true north in those situations?"

Task Versus Personal Accountability

Many organizations have become fairly sophisticated in how they measure and monitor performance. Smart goals, balanced score cards, and various types of tracking systems abound. I asked Steve why he thought executives struggle with holding each other accountable regarding personal behavior versus simply the tasks of the organization.

Steve told me, "It is trust. Trust in the other individuals, trust in yourself, and the willingness to get to the point where you are willing to give somebody else that power. Accountability on collaborative decisions is much easier because it depends upon agreement with others about particular outcomes. The decisions that get most people in trouble (the ones you read about in the paper) are made in the privacy of their own counsel. We have to invite other people in to be truly accountable.

"In my own case, I've found that when I tell others about something I am struggling with, the very nature of articulating it helps me recognize what the right decision is. You almost don't even need their verbal answer. By bringing the issue into the light of day, you often realize what the right decision is."

By bringing the issue into the light of day,
you often realize what the right decision is.

Accountability Is Personal

Steve and I talked about how certain key people at PepsiCo played a crucial role in holding him accountable. I asked him to elaborate on how this worked.

"There were two groups of people who assisted me with this challenge. One was a personal group of people to whom I had been accountable before I took the CEO position. I asked them to renew their commitment to hold me accountable in this new role. The chairman of the board of that small group of people was my wife, and we had many conversations leading up to that day. Several other lifetime friends served on my personal board of advisors.

"The second group was composed of colleagues at work. One ran the Public Relations and Public Affairs group. We had worked together for many years. He was one who I challenged to not only do his professional job well, but also to challenge me when he felt that I was heading in a direction that was inappropriate either professionally or personally or both. The other colleague was PepsiCo's General Counsel. My challenge to him was that he had veto right on any action I took. I retained the right to push back, but I promised that he had the last vote on any matters that related to my actions."

It struck me as quite significant that the leader of a major company would voluntarily place himself under the accountability of individuals lower than himself on the organization chart. I wanted to know if there were instances where they actually overruled his decisions. Did anyone actually exercise the right to veto?

It struck me as quite significant that the leader of a major company would voluntarily place himself under the accountability of individuals lower than himself on the organization chart.

"In both cases, the answer is yes. The Public Relations and Public Affairs head and I worked together almost every day. In an average week, he probably pushed back half a dozen times. We had an ongoing dialogue and he was a good sounding board.

"The general counsel's issues contained much more gravity, and he took them very seriously. When I hired the GC [General Counsel], I don't think he would have taken the job if I had not made myself accountable to him. He was that type of an individual, and that is why I chose him.

"There were at least two occasions I can remember where the GC exercised his veto. In one instance, I tried very hard to persuade him to change his mind, but he did not. He ultimately prevailed, and I valued that."

I noted to Steve that being accountable to a trusted advisor is extremely helpful, provided you are willing to be transparent. I can think of a number of examples of leaders who would not have proceeded if they had been willing to talk openly about some of their decisions. Instead they chose not to bring the issue into the light of day, and disaster ensued.

Steve commented, "There is a little adage—'You can always do something you haven't done. You can't undo something you have already done.' I have found that sometimes a pause before you say something or do something is very helpful.

"I do my best thinking in the mornings. I have learned over many, many years to sleep on it when I am wrestling with something that is of some gravity. I am not likely to make as good a decision at night as I am in the morning. Part of that is also the time to let some of those decisions percolate until true north is determined. It also gives me the time to get the counsel of a trusted advisor."

He added, "The pointer on the compasses we used when I was doing navigation in the military didn't settle quickly. Sometimes it would go back and forth; you would have to wait before you could really see the direction. In the decisions we make, it's also important to let the pointer become steady."

WHEN THERE'S NOTHING THERE

Emerging leaders who experience a dearth of accountability often want a sounding board for issues with which they are wrestling. I asked Steve what he would recommend.

"We can create our own board of advisors. I found that people like to be asked to serve in that role. Some people don't, but most do, particularly when mutual respect exists. If the accountability is not inherent in the organization, creating it is terribly important. If there are not leaders who have wisdom, experience, and age, I would look to peers that have been through the same thing for advice."

Effective leaders want feedback, but they also need to provide feedback to their followers with respect to the task and to personal behavior. I asked Steve how he handled giving feedback to those who needed to address their personal behavior.

"One of the benefits of getting older is sometimes I get a little wiser. I wish I had done this earlier in my career, but I am much more willing to take the risk of giving people feedback on sensitive areas of personal performance and personal behavior than I would have been twenty years ago. It is uncomfortable for most of us, but I know that when I am confronted by somebody, seldom am I surprised by it. You know it, and you just need somebody to push you that last piece. It also helps for you to be aware that others know about the issue, too."

OUR BIGGEST TESTS

We tend to gain wisdom when we are tested. I asked Steve about the biggest tests of integrity that he faced during his corporate career.

"The biggest tests for me were in the area of personal balance. We all want to live a balanced life. We have more responsibility to our family and to our faith than to our work. All those things are part of the character of who we are. Over my career were tests where I had to step out and deal with what was becoming an imbalance in my life. I feel very fortunate that a couple of those very difficult decisions made all the difference for our family. Retiring from PepsiCo was the biggest one. I was traveling internationally and around the country and gone constantly. I was commuting from Dallas to my office in New York.

"I had two children who were in middle school and about to enter high school. I knew that the balance wasn't right. Now that I look back at six years ago, I was dangerously close to a personal redline, probably much closer than I even knew at the time."

Steve's wife played a critical role, but I wondered if he sought the counsel of others. How did he ensure that he did not redline?

"You know it is interesting, Tim, because I did get others' counsel. It is one of the times that I ended up not taking the majority advice. The majority advice was, 'You can work through this. Don't retire.' My wife did not say that. But the other people I took counsel from all felt that it could be worked through. In that case, I am glad I did not go with majority rule."

Safeguarding Marriage Commitments

Many leadership failures occur because of extramarital affairs. This gets particularly messy when it involves another person at work, especially a subordinate. I asked Steve to comment on this.

"It is an age-old problem. I don't think it is happening more now than it has happened for hundreds and hundreds of years; however, because of the media, the ability to get away with it is not as high as it used to be. The real issue is very basic. What do I really believe? What is really important to me? We have to remind ourselves every day, several times a day—what is really important? What do I really value?

"Second, do I have balance in my life? Some of these very talented people who derail push themselves to a point where they live on a razor's edge. That is when we are more likely to make really bad decisions. We all are human, and there is a point where you cannot sustain the level of activity that is going to be optimal. Even if we have great values and commitment, when we let ourselves get so far out of balance, we are much more likely to get into trouble. This is even truer when there is no one around to pull us back."

Steve continued, "I particularly like to ask myself, 'If whatever I am considering doing was visible to everyone around me, would I still do that?' If I am at risk for not adhering to the values I know are right, that question usually catches me. I conclude, 'No, I would not do that.'

"We also have to be extremely careful about rationalization. We need clear boundaries to ensure that we do not talk ourselves into violating the values we know to be true. When leaders fail, there has to be a series of rationalizations to get to the point they do. Assuming that what we see and read in the media is true, this was certainly the case recently with General David Petraeus. He is too principled. He talked about leadership too much not to know that the path he was on was progressively leading to a bad place. Without knowing all the sordid details, you have a sense that when he started down the track well over a year ago, a slow-motion train wreck was inevitable.

"In a *New York Times* article I read, there were some significant rationalizations along the way that should have been warning signs to him. When he learned the biography was going to be written, he apparently concluded, 'If it is going to be written, I should at least try to influence it.' The amount of contact that would be needed with the author to shape the outcome should have been a warning sign. When he realized that to influence the direction of the book he would have to divulge confidential information, he should have seen a lot bigger warning flag. He also appears to have ignored the counsel of people around him. There were a whole series of what appears to be early-warning signs that went unheeded."

What Role Can a Spouse Play in Accountability?

Whenever I have spoken with Steve over the years, he frequently mentions his wife, Gail, and what an important role she plays in his personal and professional life. I asked him to comment further about how she holds him accountable.

"It starts with a relationship. We met and fell in love well before the corporate world came along. I was in the U.S. Marine Corps at the time. She didn't marry into a corporation. Her acceptance of me had nothing to do with the role I had. Because she does not get her satisfaction out of my role or level in a company and does not have a vested interest in the company, it is easier for her to be objective about what she sees and how I should act.

"She is more interested in my welfare, our welfare, and our children and family's welfare than in what I do or where I go. That takes an enormous amount of pressure off. To be able to say 'no' to a promotion was easy. If she had to choose between my being at home or having a promotion, clearly, she would rather have me home. That is foundational. We started a marriage with a set of commitments that were clear to us, and they did not have anything to do with vocational success. So if I made a decision that was not consistent with what we had agreed to, it was much easier for her to talk about that.

"Gail has a lot of wisdom and a lot of ability to envision our lives in the future. We had many conversations about balance that ultimately led to my retirement from PepsiCo. There was always a sense that, 'We are in this for the long haul so we are going to work this out. But is this right for our kids?' Our commitments provide great clarity. We knew that we didn't get a second chance in raising our kids."

Steve's Advice for Younger, Aspiring Leaders

Steve has always had an interest in the development of younger leaders. He is devoted to this end in his current role as dean of an outstanding business school. I asked him about what advice he gives to younger, aspiring leaders.

"Be clear about what you believe is important. Make sure you are fully conversant with yourself about what is success and how you are you going to measure it. How are you going to make sure that you have the highest likelihood of doing those things that lead to success? How will you have people around you to keep you accountable for the things that you say are important and to challenge you if you are not acting consistently with your beliefs? Be sure to have people around who care about you and who will challenge you," Steve says.

Every now and then I hear a politician make a comment about another elected official, saying that what a person does in his or her private life is none of our business. Any behavior on a leader's part that could tarnish the brand or credibility of an organization (or a country) is not private. Young leaders need to keep this idea firmly in place as they navigate their early years at work. Social media has an extraordinary power to make private behavior very public.

Accountability is a vital discipline for developing and protecting our core. The next chapter takes the disciplines from previous chapters and provides actionable steps to implement these disciplines. We certainly do not want to be like Jack the mule constantly walking on the edge and ready to fall off the ledge at any instant.

GO DEEPER

During my interview with Steve Reinemund he identified ten major principles for leader accountability (summarized below). Identify the three that are most relevant to you and indicate specific actions you intend to take to implement the principles you selected.

Steve Reinemund's Ten Major Principles of Leader Accountability

1. Get commitments from others to challenge you on a regular basis.

2. Prepare yourself in advance for those spontaneous, unexpected challenges to my integrity.

3. Create a personal board of directors.

4. Give veto power over contemplated actions to a respected and knowledgeable colleague.

5. Hit the pause button for important decisions any time there is a lack of clarity.

6. Conduct the visibility test—ask if whatever you are considering doing was visible to everyone around you, would you still do it?

7. Be extremely careful about rationalization—have others test your reasons for contemplated actions.

8. Heed early-warning signals, especially any sense of extreme imbalance in your work and personal lives.

9. Be clear about what you believe about success.

10. Take the risk to give followers feedback on their personal behavior.

CHAPTER 15

PILATES FOR THE LEADER—HOW TO FURTHER STRENGTHEN OUR CORE

"Great leaders must give up the force of their habits."

—SOCRATES

Anne grew up in Oregon. Her dad was an avid outdoorsman, hunting deer in the mountains and fishing for steelhead in the many coastal rivers. Despite her family's love of the outdoors, Anne developed a fear of bears. As children, Anne and her sister, Nancy, shared a bedroom. One time in the middle of the night, Anne awakened suddenly and realized that a bear had wandered into their home and was actually asleep on the floor of their bedroom between their beds. She lay terrorized beyond belief and tried to remain quiet and motionless in her bed for what seemed like an eternity. She saw the bear's blackish-brown fur rising and falling with each breath. The bear smelled, and it snored as it slept on their floor. Tears streaming down her cheeks, Anne was terrified that the bear might wake up. So paralyzing was her fear that she could not even call for help.

Although she felt completely immobilized, Anne realized that the only answer was to see if she could slip past the bear and get to her parents' room. She knew her father would get his gun and save them from the bear. Without a sound she slid under her covers to the foot of the bed. Ever so quietly she tiptoed past the huge sleeping bear. She opened the door and ran to her parents' bedroom crying hysterically for her dad. Startled from a deep sleep he ran groggily to her room and flipped on the light. There on the floor was Anne's puffy brown duvet! You can probably understand why Anne's parents sometimes referred to her as their "high strung" child. (Another unresolved family tension is that Anne has never satisfied Nancy with her explanation for why she left Nancy asleep in the room with the bear.)

Earlier in the book we established that our beliefs determine our behavior—how we feel and how we act—even if those beliefs are not true or even rational. Anne believed that a huge bear slept on her bedroom floor, and she acted accordingly, both in emotion (fear) and action (running to her dad).

When our core is breached, our beliefs become vulnerable to a host of lies, distortions, misbeliefs, and rationalizations. Protecting our core is of paramount importance if we want to have great impact as a leader. Over the course of this book, we looked at a number of disciplines to guard and develop our core. The purpose of this chapter is to make these ideas highly actionable. What should we do to sustain strong and effective leadership? Here are some actions you can start today:

DETERMINE YOUR NON-NEGOTIABLES

False beliefs love a vacuum. They move about to and fro looking for a place to lodge. If our beliefs are not carefully constructed, there are lots of competing beliefs out there only too happy to fill in the empty spaces.

Our core holds many beliefs on many subjects, some of which are subject to change based upon new information. I used to believe that abstract art was created by artists who had trouble painting something real. In fact, it is about applying paint in interesting ways using color and shapes to create visual interest. Anne has helped me understand that good nonrepresentational art is actually very difficult to create. When she told me I did not have to find something I recognized (like a barn in a snowstorm) I began to look at this art form differently. My beliefs about its artistic value changed.

Many beliefs, like my view of abstract art, are malleable, but there should be some foundational beliefs that are impregnable. We need to intentionally determine our core beliefs and ensure that they guide our behavior consistently. These few are my non-negotiables, for which I am willing to follow even at the cost of loss of favor or even loss of job. Here is a list of my personal foundational beliefs I adopted many years ago.

I believe that:

1. My primary mission in life is to honor God, live a life of integrity, and serve others in all that I do.
2. My second highest priority is to honor my family and provide for them and protect them.
3. Any accomplishments or successes I might have achieved are only because of God's grace and the help of many great people.
4. Having work I love is one of life's highest privileges. Those who provide me with an income must be served with every ounce of imagination and diligence I can muster. I do not want to coast into my retirement years. I do not want to "retire" from work until I cannot continue.
5. I have not been called to a "safe" life, in which there are no risks and all the questions are answered. I need to push against boundaries and to seek the wisdom of others to pursue new ideas.

These foundational beliefs get tested all the time, and unfortunately, I let competing misbeliefs take over from time to time, particularly when I am fatigued or excessively stressed. If you were with me for very long, you would see that my behavior often displays the disappointing consequences of violating these beliefs. My point in sharing my foundational beliefs with you is only to say that I am clear about what they are. When I am reflective and intentional, these codified beliefs guide my behavior in redemptive and fruitful directions. They give me a backdrop against which to test rival beliefs that routinely seek to enter my belief file. Goodness crowds out the bad. When I am stressed out, tired, or careless, these foundational beliefs become less accessible, and my core is more subject to being breached.

Our foundational beliefs are unique, personal, and often evolving as we learn from new experiences; however, I strongly urge you to determine what yours are. Think deeply about your beliefs and write them down. Be pithy and straightforward. This is not the place to strive for lofty language. Study your behavior and find where you regularly entertain misbeliefs that compromise your foundation. Be thoughtful and intentional about the life narrative that your foundational beliefs create. Ask yourself if this is the narrative you would want read at your funeral. Reflect on what changes you need to make. If there are areas of your life that are not working out well, look for the false beliefs that may have become lodged in your core.

CAREFULLY RECRUIT A PERSONAL BOARD OF DIRECTORS

Organizations rely on a board of directors to provide wisdom, accountability, and oversight. The board meets with the organization's leaders to provide support and encouragement, to ask them the hard questions, to hold them accountable for results and commitments, and to make sure that the organization is operating soundly.

A "personal board of directors" is a huge idea for leaders who want to make an impact in the pursuit of their aspirations. These are individuals with whom you meet periodically to discuss and to contemplate various actions. In Chapter 14 Steve Reinemund pointed out how significant this type of group had been to him during his tenure as chairman and CEO of PepsiCo.

I have such a board as well, and when I am contemplating an important decision or feeling that an action is not going as intended, I seek the advice of my trusted advisors. These individuals also provide the moral support and accountability I need to make the tough decisions and hard changes both personally and organizationally.

Often I meet with my advisors individually, not as a group. These individuals are not friends but rather are trusted advisors. Their role is to support my best interests, not to agree with me. Individuals who do well in such a role are committed to me and have the character and courage to say no. They possess the experience, discernment, and judgment to provide wise counsel, and are credible, which fosters my trust in their advice.

In assembling your own personal board, focus on finding individuals you respect and who have been around the track more times than you have. Certainly, they should understand the type of organization for which you work. Just start meeting with them occasionally and talk about the challenges you are facing. You are not asking them to join a formal organization but rather to simply spend time talking about what matters to you.

BE VERY, VERY CAREFUL WITH POWER

We discussed in Chapter 6 that leadership and power are inseparable, and, when used well, power can create great impact for good. Ungoverned power can be dangerous, as it breaches the protective walls of our core, leading to arrogance and actions that are self-serving. Of particular concern is that these effects are so subtle, we might not even know it when our core is breached. When we have power we must exercise great self-awareness, wrap it in humility, and rein in its deleterious effects.

---

*When we have power we must exercise
great self-awareness, wrap it in humility,
and rein in its deleterious effects.*

As we grow in our responsibilities and the power that often accompanies them, it becomes even more important to build containment walls. For example, Steve Reinemund explained how he asked others to help in his newly assumed role to strengthen his day-to-day accountability.

The "derailment hall of fame" is full of executives who did not manage their power well. Humility and accountability are the best anecdotes for insulating our core from the negative influences of power.

PROACTIVELY ENGAGE IN FREQUENT AND INTENTIONAL INTROSPECTION

Accessing the beliefs and convictions that govern our behavior as leaders requires we conduct a persistent, courageous, and introspective inventory. This is particularly true as our foundational beliefs evolve over time. We must also identify and detonate false beliefs and repopulate our belief system to create the narrative we intend.

Questions we must ask ourselves are: Do we believe in the value of looking inside? Are we willing to make this a way of life? I am not talking about donning a robe and walking around with a vacant, ethereal look on our faces, but rather are we willing to take time to look at our behavior and to understand ourselves? Are we willing to fumble around a bit, learning to go deeper into our core? Are we willing to submit our beliefs to rigorous self-examination? Identify any reasons that make you resistant to looking deep and try challenging those reasons. Are the risks inherent in following a path of personal destruction enough to get our attention? Why are we any different from those who went off the rails ahead of us?

In Chapter 3 I presented "Background Influences," such as family background, that shape who we are. I firmly believe that we do not have to live under the determination of what we learned earlier in our lives. We can certainly achieve escape velocity from any belief no matter how strongly entrenched it might be. We must ask, "Are we telling ourselves the truth?" We must ask if the narrative revealed in our self-talk is who we really want to become—our legacy.

LISTEN TO YOURSELF—AND TALK BACK

We must become effective at listening to our self-talk, *but not always believing it*. Our self-talk reveals the beliefs in our core, but it does not tell us which beliefs are right. We have to become effective at distinguishing the false beliefs from the true and then detonating the false ones. My work stationery has a watermark, so if I am printing a document I hold the stationery up to the light above my desk to look at the watermark to make sure I am printing on the correct side of the paper. One way to challenge our emerging beliefs is to hold them up against the light of our foundational beliefs. Ask yourself if your beliefs about a person or an opportunity are consistent with what you hold dear. If not, hit the detonation switch and replace them with beliefs that are consistent. Stopping a belief from lodging in our belief file is easier than blowing up an entrenched one.

MAINTAIN A ROBUST EARLY-WARNING SYSTEM

Most leaders headed for compromise have ample early warning to change course if they simply pay attention and heed the signals. A good rule of thumb is that if something doesn't seem right, there is a good chance it is not. Use that insight to look deeper.

Often the early warning comes in the form of feedback from others. We will likely never know for sure, but it would be revealing to know if General Petraeus had early-warning signals. Did a trusted advisor ever caution him about how much time he was spending with Ms. Broadwell? The cover story that she was interviewing him to write his biography likely did not fool everyone.

An early-warning signal should be ready to go off when we start entertaining a prospective action such as, "What would it be like to . . . [fill in the blank]?" Our "What it would be like to" mental rehearsal is closer to becoming reality than we might think, because we are toying with a new belief. When the "What it would be like to" idea violates one of our foundational beliefs, a flashing red light should go off in our heads. In the absence of a warning, we begin to entertain the false belief in earnest. The "What it would be like to" becomes "I would like to." Any foundational belief for which we lack real conviction becomes a prime target for substituting a "rational lie," in this case, "It would be okay to. . . ." We all play these mental games, but to have a positive and lasting impact as a leader, we must intercept these ideas early and detonate the false beliefs before they become lodged in our core. Also, remember to hit the pause button when there is significant ambiguity about a given action.

Run Your Personal Gallup Survey Frequently

As Steve Reinemund pointed out so well, most leaders are reluctant to provide feedback about personal behavior. People below you on the org chart are particularly reluctant to speak truth to power. Steve went to various constituents and made it clear that he needed their feedback to do his job well. He solicited their feedback. We must do the same. Feedback is vital to keeping us on course.

In asking for feedback from a trusted advisor, I have found that it helps to prime the pump. We might say, "I believe I could have handled this better if I told Sally *before the meeting* that she was coming on too strong about her idea for the new marketing campaign. As it turned out, I had to back her down during the meeting, and it made it awkward for everyone. How did you feel about that?" That invites further discussion about how you are leading the team.

It is also helpful to get feedback from multiple sources. An excellent tool used in many organizations is 360-degree feedback. This type of assessment instrument asks a number of questions about the person being rated. The questions are answered anonymously by the person's peers, subordinates, and other knowledgeable parties. Usually the person's boss also answers the questions except without anonymity. It opens wide the awareness window we talked about in Chapter 4. The first time I completed a 360-feedback exercise, I formed a panel that helped me understand the feedback results more completely. I assured the people on my panel that I was not interested in knowing how they personally rated me, but I did want their help in interpreting the feedback. My panel included direct reports who were mature and willing to be candid. The color commentary they provided on my 360-feedback results was tremendously helpful in elucidating the feedback my raters provided me.

BE YOUR OWN BEST CENSOR

Our belief file resides within our core and is subject to a host of influences. False beliefs are like dandelion seeds that float effortlessly over the wall of our core, seeking a nice place to lodge in our belief file. False beliefs lead to all kinds of errant behavior, including actions that place us at risk for catastrophic leadership failure.

False beliefs are like dandelion seeds that float effortlessly over the wall of our core, seeking a nice place to lodge in our belief file.

What parent would not exercise some discretion about movies their children see, TV programs they watch, or video games they play? Parents do this for children because their judgment has not matured enough to make good decisions for themselves. In the same way, we must "parent" ourselves and exercise good judgment about what we see and read.

I marvel at the power of media, and so I believe we have to be especially vigilant to not expose our core to anything we are not prepared to examine critically. The problem with media is that we usually watch a movie for entertainment at night when we are tired. Our defensive shields are down. There have been times when I chose to turn off movies at home or walked out of movies at the theater when I felt I did not have the mental/emotional energy to deconstruct its message thoughtfully.

Research has established the power of "modeling" in forming behavior in children. These same principles apply to adults. If we see someone who is cool and attractive, we are vulnerable to having their worldview seep into our belief system in an unconscious way. As insipid as most reality TV shows are, they can still exert subtle influences on our core.

We have to work this out however we see best, but if we want to be an effective leader who makes an impact, we cannot unthinkingly absorb the lowest common denominator values inherent in much of entertainment media. This process of being deliberately judicious includes the information media as well. We must be careful to not unthinkingly introject the ideas of writers and media journalists, even the ones we respect.

BE YOUR OWN JOURNALIST

A number of leaders with whom I meet carry a notebook with them throughout their day. Some use their iPad for the same purpose. They journal throughout the day to record what happens in meetings, phone calls, etc., as well as their thoughts and reflections about these interactions. Some of the notes concern follow-up actions, but perhaps even more important, these leaders capture what is going on inside them—their thoughts, feelings, observations, and judgments about their own work. My sense is that this is a really good idea. At the end of the day they record any insights in their journals, and turn insights into actions . . . "I will now do this." On the weekend, they review their journal and note any trends and big ideas. This is an important practice that can dramatically raise self-awareness, resulting in better self-regulation. I recommend it highly.

DISCIPLINES TO STRENGTHEN OUR CORE

When I went to college, all students were required to complete four semesters of physical education classes. Because I loved the water, I took all my PE classes in a sequence that led to certification as a Red Cross Water Safety Instructor. I worked as a lifeguard one summer, though I never had to rescue anyone. Years later I spoke at a meeting in the small coastal town of Manta, Ecuador, where locals make the famous Panama hats. One day, the conference participants had the afternoon off for recreation, so a lot of us went over to a beautiful nearby beach. After visiting with a few of the other guests, I settled back for a siesta. I awakened to the sounds of panic. People on the beach were yelling about something. When I stood up and went to the water's edge, I realized that a mother and her daughter were caught in a riptide. The strong current took them farther and farther from shore, and they were obviously in trouble. The beach did not have a lifeguard and none of the equipment our instructor taught us to use was available. I found a scraggly piece of rope and swam toward them.

By the time I arrived the two were flailing around in the water. I threw them the lifeline and pulled them parallel to the beach to get out of the riptide. Eventually with the help of a couple of other swimmers, we managed to get them to shore. The two were frightened and exhausted but relieved. (The rescue was caught on tape by a CNN reporter and shown all over the world—just kidding.)

Many people with whom I speak feel like they are in an organizational riptide. The chaos and uncertainty can be overwhelming. It is my heartfelt desire that this book proves to be a lifeline for you.

I believe that you aspire to be the kind of trusted leader who inspires others to give themselves unreservedly to your organization's mission. You also want to be able to recognize and avoid the destructive path that so many seem to take today. Of course, you also want challenge and responsibility. You hope for recognition and advancement. You desire stimulating work. I also believe that you *long to make an impact* with your life. Applying the ideas and principles in this book will help you be a leader who makes an impact—the hope of every great leader.

It is tempting to read a book like this and put it on the shelf—I often do that with even good books. The stakes are so high that I hope you will make an exception and leave this book within easy reach. My purpose in writing this book was to help you become a great leader through strengthening and protecting your core. What I have described in this book requires discipline and thoughtful application that take time, but the payoffs are extraordinary. A strong core is at the epicenter of effective leadership and resulting impact. It prevents us from going down the terrible path of personal destruction that we see so many take. The lessons conveyed throughout this book and the disciplines summarized in this chapter, when practiced, will make us dramatically better at leading.

Not only are the stakes high, but our time to make an impact is limited. The psalmist had the right perspective when he prayed, "Lord, remind me how brief my time on earth will be. Remind me that my days are numbered—how fleeting my life is."[1] I wish the very best as you build a great legacy . . . and make an impact with your life.

Please go online to www.drtimirwin.com and take advantage of the free resources. Talk with trusted advisors about how to apply these principles.

Epilogue

Let's Revisit the Story

Have you ever watched one of those movies where you could choose from a variety of endings? Remember Doug from the Prologue? Let's now assume Doug subscribed to the principles set forth in this book, in which case the narrative unfolds differently. We will pick up the scene when Doug reenters the boardroom.

Charigan's Board Chairman, Hal Barchans, greeted Doug and motioned him to the seat on his right.

"Doug, in our executive session, the board talked about the last two years. We appreciate the excellent financial results you posted this year. What we want to acknowledge even more are some of the changes you've made. As we all know, you got off to a rocky start. Your decision to centralize all operations in New York, while not without some merit, was pronounced on the organization. People thought you were power hungry and wanted to control everything. They didn't understand why you were changing something that had arguably worked extremely well for the last decade. The whole company was aware that you and Carl were really at odds over these changes. At first, you didn't win over the folks who make this company successful, and all the board heard about was mass defections on the field.

"We know that you believed strongly that we had to get control of our expenses, create some efficiencies, and eliminate a lot of the redundant systems in our regional offices. You told us that you believed the old guard was too entrenched and need to be shaken up. You made it clear to us

that you believed the only way to accomplish these ends was to centralize operations, but the amount of turbulence this created surprised us all.

"You recognized this, too, and your decision to slow down and take stock of the organization's readiness for these changes was excellent. Charigan has a long history of involving those stakeholders who are closest to our customers, which you decided to do. Going to Carl and asking for his help took some humility. We respect you for this.

"Your willingness to draw on the collective wisdom of your field leaders has borne a lot of fruit. The solution of keeping our regional sales structure, but centralizing IT, Distribution, and Accounting seems to be working out well. This year's all-employee survey affirmed you for listening and being willing to change. The organization sees you as a strong leader but also committed to getting the folks with you. By the way, it was a nice touch to feature Carl at the annual stockholder meeting. Overall, the board is pleased with the progress organizationally, and as I said before, we like the earnings report! You are making a significant impact. Congratulations! Keep up the good work."

Acknowledgments

Although one author's name appears on the cover of this book, many have contributed in some significant way. My wife's positive expectations and persistent encouragement made all the difference. As stated in the dedication of the book, she is a gifted leader and has had a profound influence on countless people's lives, most notably mine. My dear friend and colleague for many years, Pat MacMillan shaped the direction of the book in foundational ways during our numerous whiteboard sessions and through his feedback on early drafts of the manuscript. He has a truly remarkable ability to deconstruct ideas and to discover relevant truth. I want to thank my friend Steve Reinemund for providing great insight on the topic of accountability. Steve exemplifies excellence in all that he does. Thanks to Jeremie Kubicek, who influenced my early thinking about the three-faces model and encouraged me to write this book. Special appreciation to Colonel Cole Kingseed, USA (Ret.), former West Point Military Historian, who assisted me with the opening story about Colonel Chamberlain.

My literary agent, Shannon Marven, showed tremendous commitment to finding exactly the right publisher for this book. I am deeply grateful for her representation. When the publisher of BenBella Books, Inc., Glenn Yeffeth, told me that he had been looking for the right book on leadership for several years, and that he and his team believed *Impact* was that book, I knew I was home. Thanks to him for his ongoing attention to and support for the book. Editor-in-Chief Debbie Harmsen has been a great ally. She has unique gifts in making ideas clearer and the writing better. Thanks to Eric Wechter, who did an inspired job of copy editing, and Jessika Rieck for diligently overseeing the design and production process. Adrienne Lang, Deputy Publisher of BenBella Books, has shepherded this book through the publishing process adroitly.

Finally, I want to thank the many clients I have been blessed to know and to serve. I have a great appreciation for how hard they work at making their organizations excel, often under challenging market conditions and in tough competitive environments. Many of their stories illustrated the ideas in this book. I have been deeply influenced by all that I have learned from them.

NOTES

Please note that most page references relate to the location number in the Kindle version of the book.

CHAPTER 1

1. *Holy Bible*, New Living Bible Translation (Carol Stream, IL: Tyndale House Publishers Inc., 2007), King Solomon, Proverbs 4:23.
2. James R. Brann, "America's Civil War: Defense of Little Round Top," *Historynet*, last accessed September 6, 2013, www.historynet.com/americas-civil-war-defense-of-little-round-top.htm.
3. IMDb page for the film *Gettysburg*, last accessed September 6, 2013, www.imdb.com/title/tt0107007.
4. Col. Cole C. Kingseed, USA (Ret.), Professor of Military History, West Point, personal correspondence to author (August 30, 2012).
5. John Sutter, "Five Memorable Quotes from Steve Jobs," *CNN*, last modified October 6, 2011, http://articles.cnn.com/2011-10-05/tech/tech_innovation_steve-jobs-quotes_1_quotes-apple-co-founder-steve-jobs?_s=PM:TECH.

CHAPTER 2

1. http://thinkexist.com/quotation/leadership_is_a_potent_combination_of_strategy/207376.html.
2. "Mark Zuckerberg Really Does Wear the Same Thing Every Day, Cops to Owning 20 Identical T-Shirts," last modified October 3, 2012, *The Huffington Post*, last accessed September 6, 2013, www.huffingtonpost.com/2012/10/03/mark-zuckerberg-really-does-wear-same-thing-every-day_n_1935634.html.
3. Jim Plummer, "What Is Core Training?" *Functional Fitness Facts*, last accessed September 6, 2013, www.functional-fitness-facts.com/what-is-core-training.html.

4. Tim Irwin, *Derailed: Five Lessons Learned from Catastrophic Failures of Leadership* (Nashville, TN: Thomas Nelson Inc., 2009), pages 242–244.

CHAPTER 3

1. *Holy Bible*, New Living Bible Translation (Carol Stream, IL: Tyndale House Publishers Inc., 2007), King Solomon, Proverbs 27:19.

CHAPTER 4

1. Eugene H. Peterson, *The Message* (Colorado Springs, CO: NavPress Publishing Group, 2002), Proverbs 20:5.
2. Adapted from Joseph Luft and Harry Ingham, "The Johari window, a graphic model of interpersonal awareness," *Proceedings of the Western Training Laboratory in Group Development* (Los Angeles: UCLA Extension Office, 1955).
3. Rich Schapiro, "Anthony Weiner, 'future president'?: 1996 Cosmopolitan magazine named politician desirable bachelor," *Daily News*, June 7, 2011, www.nydailynews.com/news/politics/anthony-weiner-future-president-1996-cosmopolitan-magazine-named-politician-desirable-bachelor-article-1.130697.
4. ABC On Your Side, *Weiner Loses NY Mayoral Primary*, September 11, 2013, www.abc6onyourside.com/shared/news/features/top-stories/stories/wsyx_weiner-loses-ny-mayoral-primary-26162.shtml.

CHAPTER 5

1. John W. Miller and Rachel Bachman, "Paterno Ousted at Penn State," *The Wall Street Journal*, November 10, 2011, http://online.wsj.com/article/SB10001424052970204358004577027923277309662.html#printMode.
2. "Joe Paterno May Have Influenced Penn State Officials in Jerry Sandusky Cover-Up," *The Huffington Post*, last modified June 30, 2012, www.huffingtonpost.com/2012/06/30/joe-paterno-penn-state-cover-up-jerry-sandusky_n_1640074.html.
3. "National Leadership Index," *Harvard Kennedy School Center for Public Leadership*, www.centerforpublicleadership.org.

4. Alexandra Raphel, "National Leadership Index 2012: A National Study of Confidence in Leadership," *Journalist's Resource*, November 9, 2012, http://journalistsresource.org/studies/economics/business/national-leadership-index-2012#.

5. Tim Irwin, *Derailed: Five Lessons Learned from Catastrophic Failures of Leadership* (Nashville, TN: Thomas Nelson Inc., 2009), pages 25–38.

6. *Holy Bible*, New Living Bible Translation (Carol Stream, IL: Tyndale House Publishers Inc., 2007), Jeremiah 17:9.

7. IMDb page for the film *Liar Liar*, last accessed September 7, 2013, www.imdb.com/title/tt0119528/plotsummary.

8. *Macbeth*, www.bartleby.com/70/4117.html, I.vii.26–28. References are to act, scene, and line.

9. Tim Irwin, *Derailed: Five Lessons Learned from Catastrophic Failures of Leadership* (Nashville, TN: Thomas Nelson Inc., 2009), pages 139–149.

CHAPTER 6

1. "2011 Tōhoku Earthquake and Tsunami," *Wikipedia*, last modified September 3, 2013, http://en.wikipedia.org/wiki/2011_T%C5%8Dhoku_earthquake_and_tsunami.

2. France in the United States. Nuclear Energy in France. December 13, 2012. www.ambafrance-us.org/spip.php?article949

3. Nuclear Energy Institute. US Nuclear Energy Facilities Achieved Strong Safety Performance in 2012, WANO Data Shows. April 11, 2013, http://globenewswire.com/news-release/2013/04/11/537757/10028248/en/US-Nuclear-Energy-Facilities-Achieved-Strong-Safety-Performance-in-2012-WANO-Data-Shows.html.

4. Ed O'Keefe, "IRS Scandal Focus of Senate Hearing," *Washington Post*, last accessed September 7, 2013, www.washingtonpost.com/politics/irs-scandal-focus-of-senate-hearing/2013/05/21/ce4ccad4-c190-11e2-8bd8-2788030e6b44_story.html.

5. Mark Thompson, "General Disorders: Why some senior military officers are going off the rails," *Time* 180, no. 26, December 24, 2012.

6. Jonah Lehrer, "The Power Trip," *The Wall Street Journal*, August 14, 2010.

7. Philip G. Zimbardo, "Stanford Prison Experiment," last accessed September 7, 2013, http//www.prisonexp.org.

8. "Dying Woman Undergoes Additional TSA Security Screening, Says Family," *Fox News*, June 26, 2011, www.foxnews.com/us/2011/06/26/dying-woman-undergoes-additional-tsa-security-screening-says-family/.

9. Melinda Beck, "Delayed Development: 20-Somethings Blame the Brain," The *Wall Street Journal*, August 21, 2012, D1.

CHAPTER 7

1. Eugene H. Peterson, *The Message* (Colorado Springs, CO: NavPress Publishing Group, 2002), Proverbs 16:18.

2. Ben Smith, "Coakley Not Sweating It?" *Politico*, January 13, 2010, www.politico.com/blogs/bensmith/0110/Coakley_not_sweating_it.html.

3. "What Does Hubris Mean?" *InnovateUS*, last accessed September 8, 2013, www.innovateus.net/innopedia/what-does-hubris-mean.

4. *Holy Bible*, New Living Bible Translation (Carol Stream, IL: Tyndale House Publishers Inc., 2007), Obadiah 1:3.

5. Mike Volkema, Chairman of the Board, Herman Miller Inc., private conversation with author, July 22, 2009.

6. IMDb page "Quotes" for the film *Dirty Harry*, last accessed September 7, 2013, www.imdb.com/title/tt0066999/quotes.

CHAPTER 8

1. *New American Standard Bible* (La Habra, CA: The Lockman Foundation, 1960–1995), King Solomon, Proverbs 23:7.

2. "Kozlowski, Tyco Face More Questions," *CNN*, August 7, 2002, http://money.cnn.com/2002/08/07/news/companies/tyco_kozlowski/.

3. Laura Hillenbrand, *Unbroken: A World War II Story of Survival, Resilience, and Redemption* (New York, NY: Random House, 2010), pages 147–148.

4. IMDb page for the film *Indiana Jones and the Last Crusade*, last accessed September 9, 2013, www.imdb.com/title/tt0097576/.

CHAPTER 9

1. Patrick Rothfuss, *The Name of the Wind* (New York, NY: DAW Books, 2007), page 658.

CHAPTER 10

1. "Self-deception," *Dictionary.com*, last accessed September 9, 2013, http://dictionary.reference.com/browse/self-deception?s=t.

2. John Heilemann and Mark Halperin, *Game Change* (New York, NY: Harper Collins Publishers, 2010).

3. "Tiger Woods Transcript: Apology Statement Full Text," *The Huffington Post*, February 19, 2010, www.huffingtonpost.com/2010/02/19/tiger-woods-transcript-ap_n_469208.html.

4. Ibid.

5. IMDb page "Quotes" for the film *Unthinkable*, last accessed September 9, 2013, www.imdb.com/title/tt0914863/.

6. "SEC Charges Kenneth L. Lay, Enron's Former Chairman and Chief Executive Officer, with Fraud and Insider Trading," *U.S. Securities and Exchange Commission*, last modified July 8, 2004, www.sec.gov/news/press/2004-94.htm.

7. Alexei Barrionuevo, "Enron's Skilling Is Sentenced to 24 Years," *The New York Times*, October 24, 2006, www.nytimes.com/2006/10/24/business/24enron.html?pagewanted=all&_r=0.

8. "Dr. Kenneth Lee Lay," last accessed September 9, 2013, www.kenlayinfo.com.

CHAPTER 11

1. "Navy Traditions and Customs," *Naval History & Heritage Command*, last accessed September 9, 2013, www.history.navy.mil/trivia/trivia01.htm#anchor249090.

2. IMDb page "Quotes" for the film *Gettysburg*, last accessed September 9, 2013, www.imdb.com/title/tt0107007/.

3. TCM page "Quotes" for the film *Mutiny on the Bounty*, last accessed September 9, 2013, www.tcm.com/tcmdb/title/12737/Mutiny-on-the-Bounty/quotes.html.

4. IMDb page "Quotes" for the film *Crimson Tide*, last accessed September 9, 2013, www.imdb.com/title/tt0112740/.

5. Rajeev Peshawaria, *Too Many Bosses, Too Few Leaders: The Three Essential Principles You Need to Become an Extraordinary Leader* (New York,

NY: Free Press, 2011), 96. Note: Peshawaria credits Steven Kerr, former head of GE's Crotonville Leadership Development Complex, and Norman R. F. Maier, the originator of this model. Mark Miller, vice president of Chick-fil-A's Organizational Effectiveness department, also wrote about this model: Mark Miller, "The Most Powerful Leadership Equation Ever," *Great Leaders Serve* (blog), April 2, 2012, http://greatleadersserve.org/the-most-powerful-leadership-equation-ever.

6. "Introjection," *The Free Dictionary by Farlex*, last accessed September 9, 2013, http://medical-dictionary.thefreedictionary.com/introjections.

CHAPTER 12

1. Reuters, Ex-Senator Edwards acquitted on campaign finance charge. May 31, 2012, www.reuters.com/article/2012/05/31/us-usa-court-edwards-idUSBRE84T1KA20120531.

CHAPTER 13

1. *Holy Bible*, New Living Bible Translation (Carol Stream, IL: Tyndale House Publishers Inc., 2007), King Solomon, Proverbs 29:11.

2. Jonah Lehrer, "Don't! The Secret of Self-Control," *The New Yorker*, May 18, 2009, www.newyorker.com/reporting/2009/05/18/090518fa_fact_lehrer.

CHAPTER 14

1. *Holy Bible*, New Living Bible Translation (Carol Stream, IL: Tyndale House Publishers Inc., 2007), Proverbs 27:17.

CHAPTER 15

1. *Holy Bible*, New Living Bible Translation (Carol Stream, IL: Tyndale House Publishers Inc., 2007), Psalm 39:4.

ABOUT THE AUTHOR

Dr. Tim Irwin has consulted with a number of America's most well-known and respected companies. He is a frequent speaker on leadership development and other topics related to organizational effectiveness.

As an organizational psychologist and management consultant for more than twenty-five years, Dr. Irwin has assisted corporations in diverse industries, including fiber optics, real estate, financial services, baby products, information technologies, news and entertainment, insurance, hospitality, high-technology research, chemicals, sports marketing, auto parts, military optics, floor covering, bottling, quick-service restaurants, fibers and textiles, electronics, and pharmaceuticals. Dr. Irwin served from 2000 to 2005 in senior management of an international consulting firm with more than three hundred offices worldwide. Dr. Irwin's work has taken him to more than twenty foreign countries in Europe, Latin America, Africa, North America, and the Far East.

His earlier books include *Run with the Bulls without Getting Trampled* and *Derailed: Five Lessons Learned from Catastrophic Failures of Leadership*. Dr. Irwin has been a contributor on numerous national media outlets, including Fox Business News, Fox & Friends, CNBC, *The Wall Street Journal*, *Investor's Business Daily*, and *Business Week*.

Dr. Irwin received his A.B. and M.A. from the University of Georgia. His Ph.D. training included a dual major in industrial/organizational and clinical psychology from Georgia State University. He is a licensed psychologist.

Learn more at www.DrTimIrwin.com.

INDEX

Measure
Your Potential
for **Impact**

Take a **FREE** online Personal Assessment and download the Executive Discussion Guide.